KITCHENER
(BERLIN)
1880–1960

Historic Canada

Four young bucks from the Berlin area gaze across the years from 1880, and the Grand River Canoeing Club lives again. "Cook" J.A. Mowat (left) is a teacher and journalist; "purser" David Forsyth (front) is a teacher and sportsman (see page 94); and "commodore" Adolph Mueller (right) is another high school teacher. "Vice commodore" Homer Ransford Watson (back) is still recognized as one of Canada's most famous painters. For Watson, 1880 was a breakthrough year. Canada's new governor general, the Marquis of Lorne, purchased one of Watson's paintings as a gift for Queen Victoria. For the next 50 years, from his home in Doon (now part of Kitchener), Watson produced hundreds of Romantic landscapes, filling museums across Canada. His studio, near the Grand River, is now a public museum and gallery. This quartet of canoeists followed the Grand River from Breslau to Lake Erie, then to the Welland Canal. This photograph and the 40-year friendship of Forsyth and Watson, as well as that of Watson and Mackenzie King, are intriguingly analyzed in Gerald Noonan's 1997 biography of Watson, *Refining the Real Canada*, published by MLR Editions of Waterloo, Ontario. (Courtesy WHS.)

On the cover: Looking east from a balcony of the Walper Hotel, this May 1945 view shows a parade celebrating the Allied victory in Europe. (Courtesy *Record*.)

Historic
Canada

KITCHENER (BERLIN) 1880–1960

Rych Mills

ARCADIA
PUBLISHING

Copyright © 2002 by Rych Mills
ISBN 978-0-7385-1151-1

Published by Arcadia Publishing
Charleston, South Carolina

Printed in the United States of America

Library of Congress Catalog Card Number: 2002113038

For all general information contact Arcadia Publishing at:
Telephone 843-853-2070
Fax 843-853-0044
E-mail sales@arcadiapublishing.com
For customer service and orders:
Toll-Free 1-888-313-2665

Visit us on the Internet at www.arcadiapublishing.com

Author's note: All attempts have been made to notify copyright holders. Please contact the author through the Waterloo Historical Society if any omissions have occurred. Please do likewise if any further information is known about any of the images.

Harry Boehmer spent three decades cutting the hair of Berlin-Kitchener's males. From several locations around King and Queen Streets, he kept men's hair trimmed and men's ears full of the latest news. Put yourself in Harry's empty 1910 chair, make use of the "floor appliance," and join a photographic journey through 80 years of the city's history. (Courtesy WHS.)

Contents

Foreword		6
Introduction		7
1.	Some of Us	11
2.	7,829 Days	23
3.	Here and Gone	29
4.	Working for the Man	33
5.	Shop till You Drop	49
6.	Serve Us Service	61
7.	Getting Around	69
8.	Every City Has Them	77
9.	Having Fun	87
10.	Battle Lines	109
11.	Any Excuse for a Parade	119
Acknowledgments		128

Foreword

Like a voyeur, you are about to join the author at the keyhole of Kitchener. And, like voyeurs, we will not get the entire picture. This book is filled with a tantalizing, connected series of unexpected spotlights and sidebars on the famous and the unknown, the big event and the trivial, the usual and the unusual, and the incidents and coincidence of Berlin-Kitchener from 1880 to 1960. Together we will prove that what makes the past so intriguing to enter is that we never know what will happen there.

For this book, I have reversed the usual historical process. No large file of text awaited adornment by photographs; instead, the images demanded text. I headed directly to the archives of the Waterloo Historical Society and the Kitchener Public Library, where more than 10,000 photographs are held. I set the following ground rules—and usually broke them:

Each photograph had to conceal a story that could be uncovered and told. Some stories remain hidden yet.

I wanted only unpublished photographs but, in a few cases, relented to better illustrate a theme or clarify a previously published error.

There were to be only crisp, clear photographs. Please pardon those few images that are blurry, poorly composed, and over- or underexposed. The amateur snapshot can sometimes reveal a story just as well as the perfect product of a professional photographer.

Finally, I wanted a combination of images that would place the average man and woman side-by-side with the titled and famous. I believe that criterion has been upheld.

As noted in the acknowledgments, other archives and collections were certainly used, but as a Waterloo Historical Society director, I wanted to expose more of the fascinating photographs collected there over the past 90 years. And yet the more I searched, the more I lamented. How many thousands of local history photographs are lost each year through people's carelessness and forgetfulness? If this book encourages only a few people to donate to a local history archive, then its mission will be realized. Gunter Grass once wrote, in a slightly different context, "The past made me throw it in the path of the present, to make the present stumble. The future could only be understood on the basis of past made present." Present-day Kitchener is where I throw these pieces of the past—a past whose many lessons we are still learning.

I salute my friend Dorothy White Russell, who appears several times in the book. She has been a longtime inspiration and help to me, not to mention my personal link to the Victorian era into which she was born in 1900. I am happy to dedicate this book to her.

This 1925 photograph of Dorothy White Russell was taken by her husband, Clarke, in Victoria Park.

Introduction

Although a certain familiarity with Kitchener's history is a plus, my hope is that this book will also be of interest to the uninitiated, the visitor, and the newcomer. For those, I list a few points here to better enjoy this "snapshot in pictures" of the world's only sizeable community named Kitchener. At present pushing the 200,000-person mark, Kitchener lies in the centre of what used to be Waterloo Township. This, in turn, was one of several components of the old Waterloo County. Those two "Waterloos" have disappeared, replaced for the most part by the Regional Municipality of Waterloo. Since the 1860s, Kitchener has been the dominant community in the area, yet before 1916, one did not find the name anywhere.

After a reluctant beginning in the early 1800s, at a crossroads between the pioneer farmsteads of Joseph Schneider and Benjamin Eby, a tiny hamlet gradually attracted more and more newcomers through the 1820s. Harness shop, smithy, tavern, sawmill, and church—these ingredients slid into place. At some point in time, not then considered noteworthy, a name was given to the hamlet. In the mid-1820s, perhaps as late as 1833, this place was named Berlin. Local historians have long claimed, without evidence, that this was to honour the Prussian city of Berlin. However, very few 1820s immigrants of Germanic origin came from northern German states, such as Prussia. At this time, Berlin, Prussia, was not a city of great importance. Recent studies offer a second possibility. Many original settlers came here from Pennsylvania, moving north for various reasons. Pennsylvania had communities named Berlin, and it is reasonable to consider that newcomers may have brought that name with them, as they had numerous others. This nebulous beginning of Berlin's name is ironic in light of what was to happen in 1916.

By the early 1850s, Berlin boasted 700 residents. Within Waterloo County, only Galt, to the south, was growing more rapidly than Berlin. Two 1850s developments ensured that Berlin surpassed its rival. When Waterloo County was formed in 1851, an immediate battle took place between Galt and Berlin to become county seat. Berlin may have been smaller, but it included men more skilled in the ensuing political games. Eventually, the prize—county offices, courthouse, and jail—went to Berlin. The second factor was the railroad. In 1856, when the Grand Trunk Railway pushed its way west from Toronto to Georgetown to Guelph to Berlin to Stratford to London and to points west, the new county seat became linked to the world. Berlin's future was assured. It gained town status in 1871, just as the Franco-Prussian War ended in Europe. The subsequent creation of the nation of Germany from the many smaller states provided some, though not all, of Berlin's Germanic citizens with a source of pride. How Berlin grew and prospered, due largely to its unique situation as an enclave of German-speaking people, is told in fascinating detail in *Kitchener: An Illustrated History*, by John English and Kenneth McLaughlin.

By 1880, Berlin had nearly 4,000 residents and sat in the middle of some of the richest and best-managed farmlands in Ontario. To the town's northwest, another community was rising: the village of Waterloo. Eventually, the term Kitchener-Waterloo would roll off the tongue almost as a single word. Both municipalities grew rapidly and shared the nickname "Twin Cities" even before Berlin gained city status in 1912. Waterloo followed suit in 1948. Today, the two cities are intermingled in many ways and share a long, rambling boundary that literally runs through living rooms, businesses, parks, a graveyard, and even splits a golf course. For most citizens, the two cities represent different lifestyles, ethics, concerns, and most of all, traditions.

"Busy Berlin," coined as a catchphrase in the 1890s, describes perfectly the bustling, industrious, ever-growing town. As the centuries changed in 1901 and Queen Victoria died, the dawning 20th century seemed Berlin's for the taking. Businesses earned reputations throughout North America and the British Empire. Citizens spread through the land, helping to populate and develop the Canadian West. Others took their faith and headed to just-opened corners of Africa and Asia. The reality of life in Berlin before World War I seems, in retrospect, the ideal of what bilingual multiculturalism should be. Within a framework of British constitutional government, justice, and capitalism thrived the determination, drive, inventiveness, and industry of the Germanic tradition. The babble of Pennsylvania-Dutch, Scots-burr, high and low German, Yankee twang, and ruling-class English blended easily in the shops and churches, schools and factories, and playgrounds and offices of Busy Berlin.

And then it all crashed to earth between 1914 and 1919.

War, when it arrived in August 1914, was not unexpected. What was a complete surprise in Berlin was how rapidly the facade of integration was ripped away. Unlike previous wars, this one quickly affected the home fronts of participating countries. In Canada, nationally, strict censorship controlled newspapers. Provincially, German-language instruction in schools was forbidden. Locally, three militia members toppled the bust of Kaiser Wilhelm I. Most Berliners who enlisted in 1914 and 1915 were of British background; those of German extraction, even several generations back, seemed reluctant. In fall 1915, Ottawa authorized a locally raised overseas battalion, the 118th, and problems increased. Initial recruiting left the 118th understrength, and soon, undisciplined soldiers and noncommissioned officers prowled the streets, press-ganging "slackers." Then, in early 1916, the board of trade suggested changing the city's name to counter anti-Berlin sentiment across Canada. Citizens took sides, often disagreeing even within families. Prominent businessmen exchanged vicious letters in the newspapers. An outspoken German-American minister proclaimed his pride in his German-ness and was beaten. Victoria Park's pavilion was burned down. The kaiser's bust, stored at the Concordia Society hall, was again stolen. Opponents to the name change were confronted (and sometimes attacked) by mobs of soldiers and civilians. In May 1916, the 118th was posted to London, Ontario, for training, and things simmered down a bit.

The name change went through, and as the word "Berlin" was cast aside, another emerged from a deceptive and disputed voting process: "Kitchener." World War I put forth few public figures of heroic stature, but one who did stand tall was Horatio Herbert Kitchener, first Earl of Khartoum. In 1916, he was better known as Lord Kitchener, Great Britain's minister of war. Perhaps more than any single person, he was responsible for Allied victory. Kitchener was the lone leader to realize that this would be a long, wasteful war. This view, unpopular with his cabinet cohorts, prevailed, and a campaign to fill "Kitchener's Armies," promoted by the famous poster featuring his steely visage, succeeded. A year later, these armies held back what may have been a war-ending German thrust into Paris and beyond. The public still venerated Lord Kitchener in 1916, and his name was suggested as a replacement even before his death in June of that year. Berlin became Kitchener on September 1, 1916.

More trouble loomed. On civic election day, January 1, 1917, there was violence as two groups contended for council seats. The Citizen's League, accused of being pro-German, won a majority along with the mayor's chair. The mobs were out again, smashing the newspaper office and beating some successful candidates. Outside troops from nearby Galt were called in to quell the disturbance. Later in 1917, during Canada's divisive conscription election, Prime Minister Robert Borden was hooted from a local stage. A former mayor, W.D. Euler, won the riding on a strong anti-conscriptionist platform.

The hatred and mistrust of wartime strained relations among residents for a few years, but in the 1920s, the healing sped up as Kitchener regained its pre-war growth figures. Population increased by 10,000 in just 10 years, becoming 30,000 by 1930, while new industry and housing began encircling the old city. In the core, new factories joined or replaced the old. Their smoke blanketed the heart of the city, and these factories churned out rubber, felt, buttons, furniture, electrical goods, leather, tires, mattresses, and luggage—products proudly carrying the name "Kitchener" where "Berlin" had previously gone.

The Great Depression hit Kitchener hard, as it did most communities. Efforts were made to provide relief for families. A winter hostel for unemployed transients was set up in the new swimming pool's change rooms. The stunning Rockway Gardens was a make-work relief project that continues to benefit the city today. Then, once again, European matters intruded into this mid-sized Canadian city. This time, however, no hint of sympathy existed for the enemy. The city was too busy turning out wartime goods and sending its young men and women off to war.

In the late 1940s, Kitchener was growing exponentially. New suburbs overflowed adjacent township agricultural land. New businesses, industries, schools, churches, and parks were added to the inventory. Life in the 1950s was good for citizens of Kitchener. Those returning from the service had married, moved to the new subdivisions, raised their families, climbed the ladder in business, and, to steal a phrase, lived the "Kitchener Dream." There was little evidence of post-war rancour this time around.

Heading into 1960, the first edge of the baby boom moved Kitchener into the ranks of Canada's fastest growing communities. In the 15 quick years between the conclusion of the war and the end of this book's mandate, Kitchener's population doubled. What had taken 140 years to reach took only a decade and a half to reproduce.

By 1960, problems lurking below the surface became more evident. The downtown, which now requires constant priming, began losing its role as the city's shopping centre to, well, the shopping centres. Core schools saw the beginning of a shrinking student base; now several are closed. Social problems common to any large population started to invade Kitchener as the largest area community. Environmental problems previously not understood or hidden away have crept to the surface. Yes, 1960 is a turning point, and a point to turn away from for this book. We leave the next 80-year period of Kitchener to the writers and editors of 2040.

Many stories are buried within the images of this "snapshot in pictures," so come enjoy *Kitchener (Berlin): 1880–1960.*

—Rych Mills
November 2002

Mid-week in a mid-sized city in mid-century, Kitchener's new trolleys ply King Street while shoppers crowd the sidewalks. The *Record*'s photographer has captured a classic view of the rapidly growing post-war city. This view, taken from the Hotel Kitchener at Benton Street, looks west to a row of shops including Becker's Jewellery, Sehl Hardware, Miller and Hohmeier Dry Goods, Ed Heller Jewellers, the Central Tobacco Shop, and Schmidt, Dickey Drugs. (Courtesy WHS, *Record*.)

Famous throughout the British Empire well before war broke out, Lord Kitchener's near-mythical status was greatly strengthened during 1914 and 1915. In addition to the famous recruiting poster, his image appeared regularly in the world's newspapers, in magazines, and on innumerable souvenir items. Both before and after his death, millions of postcards, sent to all corners of the globe, helped establish Kitchener as the most recognizable figure of World War I. (Published by Rotary Photo; author's collection.)

One

SOME OF US

Kitchener became famous in the late 20th century for its Oktoberfest. In 1896, Berliners put on a somewhat different October festival. The Kirmes ran from October 1 to 10 and featured a traditional German village re-created in the Gaukel Street rink. Music, costumes, prizes, games, good food, and heady brew attracted some 25,000 visitors over the nine evenings. Even the cleanup crew took on a traditional role, using brand-new Made-in-Berlin brooms. (Photograph by A.S. Green; courtesy *Record*.)

Ernest John Stewart (above) was one of the first to take up bicycling on Berlin's muddy streets. A clerk at Merchants Bank, he married Martha Fennell in 1894. Her father, John Fennell, set up one of the first hardware stores in Berlin and was heavily involved in civic life as the board of trade president, the founding director of the hospital, and an organizer of the Economical Fire Insurance Company. Martha and Ernest's children were Martha (below, left), the eldest, and Ruth Marie (below, right), who married Ernest Barrie, later prominent in the city's military circles. (Courtesy KPL.)

Cars presented no problem for road hockey players in 1905. Viola and Paul Snyder took over the corner of Lancaster and Bingeman Streets beside their home but paused long enough for their father, Albert, to capture the action. Viola taught for many years at J.F. Carmichael School, and Paul worked for the Public Utilities Commission. The two reappear throughout this book. (Courtesy WHS, Sokvitne.)

Joseph Schneider was one of those hardy Mennonites from Pennsylvania who trekked to Waterloo Township in 1807. His land, Lot 17, took in most of today's downtown, and his sawmill was the first business venture in the area. The Joseph Schneider Haus and Museum now re-creates mid-19th-century life in his 1816 pioneer home. Joseph's great-great-granddaughter Martha Snyder plays near the homestead in 1908. She was the cousin of Viola and Paul Snyder, shown in the preceding photograph. (Courtesy WHS, Sokvitne.)

The Breithaupt Leather Company was the first industry to make the village's name nationally known. Louis Breithaupt of Buffalo, New York, married Berliner Catherine Hailer and began business operations in 1857. Twenty-five years later, Louis died, but under Catharine and the sons, the business flourished. Louis was a Berlin mayor and has set a family standard—at least three sons, two grandsons, and a great-grandson have held political office. Above, Catherine and son Louis J. leave the tannery and head for town in the 1880s. Below, four decades later, a brand-new Breithaupt Leather Company truck hauls hides to the tannery. (Above, courtesy BHC, UW; below, photograph by Ernest Denton, courtesy BHC, UW.)

William H. Breithaupt spent his youth in Berlin until his bridge engineering skills took him around the continent working for various railways. His wanderlust abated in 1900, when he resettled in Berlin to, among other things, run the Berlin and Waterloo Street Railway. W.H., son of Louis and Catherine, was a visionary, and his interests in planning, conservation, and hydroelectric power helped lay the groundwork for area projects in those fields. Local historians recall him fondly. With his friend Rev. Theobald Spetz, W.H. Breithaupt founded the Waterloo Historical Society in 1912. (Courtesy BHC, UW.)

W.H. Breithaupt's large home was west bookend to a string of substantial houses of prominent Berliners along Margaret Avenue between Queen and Victoria. His wife, Martha Cunningham Murphy, raised three children here while W.H. ran his business and served on the planning commission, library board, and historical groups. (Courtesy WHS.)

Berlin's Renaissance man was William H. Schmalz, businessman, politician, artist, collector, musician, historian, gardener, sportsman, and administrator (see page 123). Born in 1862, he attended the Central Public School and Berlin High School before beginning his 55-year insurance career, which culminated in the position of managing director of Economical Mutual. This c. 1885 tintype is in the collection of the Waterloo Historical Society, which Schmalz helped to found. (Courtesy WHS.)

This July 20, 1915 Knights of Pythias picnic photograph was taken at the Rumpel home on Cameron Street and contains a hidden tale. Among the faces that can be identified looms a mythical figure. Carl "Big Charlie" Pritschau literally stood head and shoulders above the rest of the population. For a decade, Pritschau had dealt in real estate and built subdivisions. He forged a "friendly giant" reputation, borrowing and loaning tens of thousands of dollars. Suddenly, in mid-summer 1920, he disappeared. Numerous small investors were left with worthless notes. Circumstantial evidence pointed to Big Charlie fleeing back to Germany, but nothing was ever heard from him. Also shown is George "Pop" Philip (seated ninth from the left with a long white tie), who will reappear in this book. (Courtesy WHS.)

Roland Shoemaker was born in Berlin in 1874. As a young man, he left town and moved west. Earlier, a brief visit to the Dominion Photographic Gallery in the Canadian Block at King and Ontario Streets gave the photographer a chance to develop his whims. Shoemaker's Berlin career as a shirtcuff salesman failed despite his claim to work twice as hard as any man. (Courtesy KPL.)

"In his novels, Millar resolved his contradictions. . . . These singular works changed their genre," writes biographer Tom Nolan of Ross Macdonald. "Ross Macdonald" served as the pen name of Kitchener's literary giant, Kenneth Millar. Beside him is Margaret Sturm Millar, a Kitchener native and a mayor's daughter. They met in the early 1930s and both worked on the high school yearbook, *The Grumbler*. From their California home in the 1940s through the 1980s, a steady stream of novels by Ross Macdonald and Margaret Millar kept millions spellbound. Their Kitchener roots are well detailed in Tom Nolan's 1999 biography. Their daughter Linda, shown at age nine in 1948 during a family visit to Kitchener, died tragically in 1971. (Courtesy *Record*, UW.)

Sattler's Leather Shop spans the decades of this book and was located on Queen Street South. Living above the shop, Louis and Louisa Sattler raised several children, including Walter and Rufus. As these 1900 and 1903 photographs show, the boys were not long in becoming handymen. Rufus (on the right in both photographs) took over the business after his father's death in 1924 and kept it running until the 1970s. (Courtesy WHS.)

18

J.M. Staebler strode through the history of Berlin and left his stamp all over it. Trained as a painter, he next opened a stationery shop and then embarked on the burgeoning button business. In his mid-50s, he changed gears again and began a still-operating insurance firm. Staebler served the town as mayor, alderman, assessor, park board member, and hospital commissioner and sat on the sewer, finance, and works committees. Probably his most enduring civic accomplishment was his early and tireless promotion of a new park: Victoria. This portrait (right), by Preston's famous James Esson, captures a young J.M. Staebler *c*. 1885. Buena Vista (below), when Staebler built it in the late 1870s, must have indeed had a good view. It commanded a panorama of forest, farm fields, and wetlands. The stately home still stands on Queen Street South, near Courtland. Just a few metres south, near that pine tree to the right, pioneer Joseph Schneider had erected his first cabin in 1807. Among later owners of Buena Vista was meat packer J.M. Schneider. (Above, courtesy WHS; below, courtesy WHS, from *The Illustrated Atlas of the County of Waterloo*, published by Parsell and Company in 1881.)

The story of J.M. Schneider making sausage in his mother's kitchen, thus founding the famous company, is well told in local history books. Here, the focus is on one of the next generation: Norman C. Schneider. Born in 1888, he apprenticed with the Tuerk Engine Company. His father's sausage business expanded, and Norman joined just in time to oversee the important step up to electrically operated, mechanical refrigeration. Eventually, Norman and his brother Fred helped make the J.M. Schneider name famous from coast to coast. Norman and his wife, Ethel (Lapsley) Schneider (see page 114), built a cottage near Freeport. Gathered at the cottage c. 1935 are, from left to right, J.M. Schneider, George Buck, Emma Buck, Louise Ahrens, Helena Ahrens Schneider (J.M.'s wife), Ethel Schneider, and Clara Lapsley. Norman's chair is empty; as usual, he took the photograph. (Courtesy Betty and Herb Schneider.)

A 1910 postcard captures two of J.M.'s sons in the front seat, Norman (left) and Fred, taking their father's Pope Hartford car out for a spin. Norman's knack for mechanics kept this and all subsequent cars in top shape. His taste for speed led him to build his first motorcycle in 1912 and to keep riding them until his mid-80s. Seated in the back are pals Carl Ahrens (left) and Walter Zeller. (Courtesy Betty and Herb Schneider.)

Left: Norman Schneider held many roles. He was an award-winning photographer, a founding member of both the old Lexington Airport and the newer one at Breslau (where the terminal bears his name), a charter supporter of Doon Pioneer Village, and a board member of the University of Waterloo. Here, he follows the news at his 76 Schneider Avenue home in 1938. (Courtesy Betty and Herb Schneider.) *Right:* In 1952, Louis O. Breithaupt, member of parliament (MP) for North Waterloo, was named Ontario's lieutenant-governor. The Liberals needed a strong figure to maintain their 35-year grip on the riding. Norman Schneider was tapped and took the subsequent by-election. He won again in 1953 and 1957 but was swept aside in the Diefenbaker landslide of 1958. He died in 1985. (Author's collection.)

"[We cater to] discriminating shoppers who demand quality merchandise at popular prices." With those words, Walter Zeller announced that Kitchener, despite the worsening depression in 1932, was to be the site for the first expansion of the new chain of Zellers thrift stores. Zeller, seen here in 1910, was born on a farm at Breslau in 1890 but grew up on Berlin's Water Street South. Who could have guessed that three of the chums in the car on the opposite page would see their surnames become Canadian household phrases through much of the 20th century? (Courtesy Betty and Herb Schneider.)

The year 1960 was a watershed year in Kitchener history, especially for ice-cream aficionados. Tyson's—for 55 years a hallowed spot—was closing. Four decades on, people still talk about the sundaes, banana splits, and tin roofs created by Olive Tyson. From a converted home at 42 Ontario North, with no chrome, no jukebox, and no other food on the menu, Tyson's served generations of sweet tooths. Olive's great-great-grandfather built the house in 1865 while operating his King Street grocery store. Olive's mother, Catharine, started selling ice cream from the grocery store as a summer sideline. The fad caught on, and in 1905, the shop opened year-round on Ontario Street. (Courtesy *Record*, UW.)

Psychologically daunting perhaps, the menu at Tyson's was handwritten on mirrors in the home's front rooms, which made up the actual ice cream parlor. Fifteen cents bought a chocolate mallow, butterscotch walnut, or black cherry sundae. Add a nickel and enjoy a chocolate mallow cashew or fresh raspberry. Only vanilla ice cream was served; it was Olive's artistry with toppings that made the difference—that and the secret Tyson ice-cream recipe. (Courtesy *Record*, UW.)

Two

7,829 Days

A crucial point in Canadian politics occurred on September 24, 1908, in Berlin's Victoria Park. A federal election campaign was under way, and the ruling Liberal party had recruited a young, rising star. Hometown boy William Lyon Mackenzie King returned to Berlin with Prime Minister Sir Wilfrid Laurier at his side. Together they brought the crowd of 10,000 to a frenzy pitch. For the 34-year-old King, it was the first public speech of his political career. For Canada, it was the first public display by the man who dominated its political world until mid-century. From his close-up position as a member of the Berlin Musical Society Band, W.H. Schmalz took this iconic photograph of the future prime minister. (Courtesy WHS.)

W. L. Mackenzie King, M. P.
"THE MAN OF THE FUTURE"

With his close victory over Conservative Richard Reid, Mackenzie King became one of Canada's youngest members of parliament ever. Six months later, his fondest dream came true: Laurier created a new cabinet post, minister of labour, and named King. The job lasted less than two years, as the Liberals were tossed from office in the 1911 reciprocity election and W.G. Weichel returned North Waterloo to the Conservatives. W.D. Euler and King were schoolmates at Central School, where Euler later taught (see page 83). Beginning his public service early, Euler sat on the school board and the city council and served as mayor. In 1917, he ended Weichel's Ottawa career, recapturing the riding for the Liberals. It was the first of seven straight federal victories, a string that catapulted him to the cabinet and senate. During King's first visit to Kitchener as prime minister in 1922, an informal snapshot at the Euler home on Queen Street North (below) catches, from left to right, W.G. Weichel, Harvey Sims, London MP W. Elliott, King, Carl Kranz, Euler, and Archie Lockhart. (Above, author's collection, published by F.I. Weaver of Berlin; below, courtesy Joan and John Euler.)

Kitchener's Old Boys and Girls Reunion in August 1925 welcomed back its most famous son. King had been prime minister for over three years, and most citizens felt pride that one of their own was running the country. From the steps of Kitchener's new city hall, King addresses the throng. Moments later, he unveiled a portrait of himself inside the building. That same portrait now hangs in a new city hall. (Courtesy WHS.)

In addition to several public visits to Kitchener as prime minister, King made numerous private trips to see friends such as the Eulers, the Honsbergers, the Breithaupts, and the Bowlbys. Perhaps his closest personal friend was Harvey Sims, who had rallied support behind the scenes in King's early campaigns. In this mid-1930s photograph at the Sims family home near Chicopee, Harvey is the tall man in the centre, and King appears to his right. Harvey's son Ken is at the far right. (Courtesy WHS.)

A defining moment in Kitchener's history occurred on June 6, 1939, when King George VI and Queen Elizabeth visited briefly. The shy, reluctant king, so different from his older brother Edward and from his personable, outgoing queen, struck a note of tradition in a world that knew it was marching towards war. Joining the royal couple on the platform for their quarter-hour stay were, from left to right, Mayor George Gordon, his wife, and Mackenzie King. The rest of the Twin Cities was virtually deserted, as schools, factories, shops, and offices closed for the day. (Courtesy WHS, *Record*.)

Prior to the 1945 election campaign, Mackenzie King had said it would be his last. As a coda to his political career, which had started in Berlin four decades earlier, a farewell visit was arranged for September 1947. Again, the turnout was huge. These two photographs capture King stepping out of a car with North Waterloo MP Louis O. Breithaupt (in the light suit) and walking down Frederick Street with Mayor J.G. Brown (dark suit). (Courtesy Murray Fried.)

During festivities at city hall on September 8, 1947, the prime minister delighted in presenting special citizenship certificates to a number of county youngsters. Following a speech on good citizenship, King invited 11 recipients forward. Dressed in her Princess Margaret Rose tartan, Marie Good of Simeon Street so charmed the prime minister that he kissed her and then a second time at the photographer's request. (Courtesy *Record*, UW.)

A vast crowd of schoolchildren fills City Hall Square. As the ageing prime minister faces them, does his mind look past the Hotel Kitchener across the street and travel one block farther south to the Benton Street site where he was born almost 74 years earlier? Imagine what memories must flood through William Lyon Mackenzie King this September 1947 during his final hometown visit. Within three years, he was dead. (Courtesy *Record*.)

On a stormy December 17, 1874, this frame cottage witnessed a birth. Berlin had many births in those days but none with so profound an effect on the history of the community, the country, and the world. The infant was given his maternal grandfather's full name, William Lyon Mackenzie, and his father's surname, King. That four-barrelled name was to be preceded by the title of prime minister of Canada for 7,829 days, longer by far than anyone else. By 1926, the house was in this sad condition and was torn down without protest to make way for a Pentecostal church tabernacle. The Waterloo Historical Society commissioned Kitchener photographer Ernest Denton to take this final view of the site. (Courtesy WHS.)

The home that King most remembered, the one most associated with him, was rented by the family from 1886 to 1893. Woodside was on the edge of Berlin in a bucolic setting that, to this day, retains little corners of mystic charm. After his retirement in 1948, King reluctantly went along with plans by local Liberals to restore Woodside, seen here in the 1950s. It is now a National Historic Site paying tribute to Mackenzie King and his family, as well as portraying 1890s middle-class life. (Courtesy Woodside National Historic Site, Parks Canada.)

Three

HERE AND GONE

Kitchener welcomed its second prime minister in less than two years when Mackenzie King's successor, Louis St. Laurent, absorbed the cheers of a 1949 city hall crowd. Members of the Kitchener Musical Society Band, led by George Ziegler (left, arm in air), join the salute. Just to George's right is future city councillor Mike Wagner. If it did not, the band should have played "St. Louis Blues" because, in addition to Prime Minister Louis St. Laurent, the car contains Louis O. Breithaupt, MP, and, driving, his son Louis P. (Courtesy Laverne Hett, *Record*.)

Not all special visitors were elected or titled—Vienna's Anton Hanslian, for instance, who dropped by c. 1908. He just happened to be walking around the world, pushing his wife and daughter on a trek that had begun in September 1900. They came and went, but their memory lingers on in Berlin, thanks to Albert Snyder, whose camera caught them in front of the Grand Central Hotel at King and Benton Streets. (Courtesy WHS, Sokvitne.)

Prince Louis of Battenberg, Germany, married one of Queen Victoria's granddaughters and rose to the top of the British navy. Visiting Toronto, he was invited to meet some former countrymen now living nearby. After lunch at the Berlin Club on the second storey of 34 King Street East, he addressed the crowd and enjoyed music by the town band. Prince Louis's son, Earl Mountbatten of Burma, also became an admiral, then the supreme allied commander in southeast Asia, and the final viceroy of India. (Courtesy Dave Moore.)

June 13, 1918. Duke of Devonshire and party Luncheon at Grand River Country Club

In June 1918, an interminable war dragged on, and Canada was still trying to heal wounds from the divisive election of 1917. What could better boost sagging spirits than a tour by the popular governor general, the Duke of Devonshire, and his two attractive daughters? Following an official reception in Victoria Park, the party toured Kitchener and Waterloo and then headed towards Bridgeport, where luncheon was served at the Grand River Country Club. That is where Ernest Denton caught this moment. (Courtesy WHS.)

Most of Kitchener-Waterloo's citizens were in the vicinity of the train station on June 6, 1939, when the royal train stopped (see page 26). A newspaper report of the time noted that thousands of photographs had been taken in the 15-minute visit. This one was snapped by Dorothy Russell, highlighting the exuberance of Queen Elizabeth and the nervousness of King George. (Courtesy Dorothy Russell.)

Another governor general who visited Kitchener was the desert war hero Viscount Alexander of Tunis. One of his duties on May 31, 1947, was to officiate at the grand opening of the new Royal Canadian Legion Hall on Ontario Street. (Courtesy WHS, Moffett.)

Led by the combined bands of Kitchener, Preston, and Waterloo, the world-famous Band of the Irish Guards visited Kitchener on October 2, 1954. (Courtesy Laverne Hett, *Record*.)

Four

WORKING FOR THE MAN

Berlin became Busy Berlin because of the successful wooing of out-of-town businesses and the steady growth of its local firms. Of the latter, McBrine Luggage was a prime example. Started in 1892 on a shoestring by Louis McBrine and William G. Cleghorn, the firm made travelling bags so well that within 10 years, this three-storey factory was built on Water Street South at Charles. At one time, McBrine bags, trunks, and luggage were known throughout the world. Some 250 employees worked at the plant in the good years, which ended when the firm closed in 1969. The factory was demolished to make way for the King Center parking garage. (Courtesy Dave Moore.)

33

Contrast this pair of photographs with the next. Where would you rather work? Another famous business founded in Berlin started in 1915 as the Metcalfe Candy Company. Just after World War II, it became Smiles 'n Chuckles. This 1925 view (above) details just how "handmade" the candies were. What job could be sweeter? Working in a bright, airy, uncrowded building, the women at Lang's Shirt Factory at 122 Victoria South (below) appear to have ideal conditions. Lang's was just one of several local shirt manufacturers and a mid-sized firm that never quite made it to the big leagues with Forsyth and Arrow. (Above, courtesy Dave Moore; below, courtesy WHS.)

In the Waterloo Historical Society collection is a remarkable series of 10 images focusing on the Brown and Erb Company at King and Gaukel. Instead of cleaned-up publicity scenes, this set portrays the nitty-gritty of a tannery and mattress factory. Young boys in the mattress-stuffing workshop (above) are overseen by a not-much-older foreman. In the tannery (below), the damp, the smell, the eye-stinging chemicals jump out of the photograph across 100 years. Not to pick on Brown and Erb for particularly poor working conditions, this picture rather shows what was acceptable everywhere c. 1900. (Courtesy WHS.)

Kitchener's sole remaining furniture factory from Busy Berlin is still at its original site, Breithaupt and Ahrens. Hartman Krug's initial 1880 efforts centred on a small building. By 1908, however, a four-storey factory was in operation and that remains today. Krug survived by specializing in finely crafted furniture. At the intersection, note Smola's Confectionery and the motorcycle officer. In this 1930s image, the train station appears in the lower right corner. (Courtesy WHS.)

Many industries were built along the railroad between King and Lancaster Streets. Behind the train station was Berlin Furniture, which later became Jacques, and still later, Galloway. This mid-1920s view looks from the station grounds past Jacques Furniture towards Victoria Street. One special streetcar, designated Royal Mail, connected the downtown post office and the railway station. (Courtesy WHS, NAC.)

Across from the station on Weber Street stood Hydro City Shoes, operated by the Detweiler brothers, with Noah (wearing glasses) in charge. Daniel, though more famous, had a lesser role. Two other brothers worked in the plant; in this c. 1920 photograph, Aaron appears third from the left, and Jacob appears second from the right. What began in 1899 as G.V. Oberholtzer Shoes was altered in 1916, anticipating the citizens would select Hydro City to replace Berlin in the upcoming name-change vote. What a surprise when Kitchener won! However, the company stuck to its choice until closing in the late 1960s. (Courtesy KPL.)

Not all small businesses grew and prospered with the changing times. Louis Timm on King Street East opposite Scott Street advertised his shop as "Manufacturers of Fine Buggies, Carriages, Sleighs &c. Painting, Shoeing, Jobbing." Timm also reportedly constructed the first town ambulance. The fire chief in the 1890s, he died at age 39 in 1905, and his business closed. (Courtesy Marg Eaton.)

At the beginning of the 20th century, dreams of sugar plum fairies mobilized a large segment of Busy Berlin. An American beet sugar producer was interested in expanding into Ontario, so the board of trade swung into action. Even dangling a voter-approved $25,000 bonus and a 10-year tax exemption, the board still came up short until stock of $100,000 was pledged. By 1902, the Ontario Sugar Company, headed by S.J. Williams, was up and running. Farmers planted sugar beets, natives from the Six Nations Reserve came up for the harvest, and top-quality sugar flowed from the factory. All was well—for a few years. By January 1909, the company was broke, the factory sold, and the dream dead. Taxpayers still had 20 years to pay on the bonus debentures, and investors received no return. The impressive industrial structure was located on Lancaster Street between Berlin and Bridgeport. The filter press room (above) was only one of a dozen steps in the sugar-making process. The imposing factory was well serviced by W.H. Breithaupt's Berlin and Bridgeport streetcars (below). (Above, photograph by James Topley, courtesy WHS, NAC; below, courtesy WHS.)

Following the 1909 bankruptcy, new owners operated the plant as the Dominion Sugar Company. The process required a great deal of water, so it was no accident that the factory was close to the Grand River. A pump house and filtration plant (above) was constructed, and its foundations remain, just downstream from Bridgeport. A portion of the original sugar factory now houses the Brown Steel Company. S.J. Williams ran Ontario Sugar but is better remembered as the W in W.G. & R. Berlin's bonuses and tax exemptions lured several outside concerns, such as the Williams, Greene and Rome Shirt and Collar Company of Toronto. Tempted by a $3,000 bonus and tax-free status, the firm moved into the vacant Vogelsang Button factory at Queen South and Courtland. The building (shown below during the late 1890s) has had many tenants, including the military in World War I, and MacDonald Electric. It is now Bread and Roses Housing Co-operative. (Above, author's collection; below, courtesy Dave Moore.)

From a series of c. 1905 photographs taken at the Williams, Greene and Rome factory are the following four interiors. In the photograph above, women work in the collar room under the eye of foreman Fred Reck on the well-lit second floor. Intense competition for working women existed among Berlin industries, so Williams, Greene and Rome decided to use working conditions and extra benefits to attract employees. Company-sponsored events, picnics, and entertainments occurred on a regular basis. Few men were employed at the company. One was Joe Shepherd, seen below in his cozy, decorated boiler room. (Courtesy KPL.)

Because many workers could not go home each noon for good meals, Williams, Greene and Rome operated its dining room (above) as a fine restaurant. Morale-boosting entertainments were arranged, consisting of skits, excursions, and improvement lectures. The employee library (below) was well stocked with books, newspapers, and writing materials. Deputy Minister of Labour Mackenzie King, visiting Berlin one summer day in 1907, found the innovative firm shut; his disappointment turned to delight when he learned it was so that Williams, Greene and Rome workers could enjoy two weeks of vacation, just as the managers did. (Courtesy KPL.)

THE WILLIAMS, GREENE & ROME CO., LTD.

MAKERS OF FINE SHIRTS, COLLARS, PYJAMAS
BOYS' BLOUSES AND SUMMER UNDERWEAR

FACTORY AND HEAD OFFICE
KITCHENER

MONTREAL　　TORONTO　　WINNIPEG　　VANCOUVER

As Berlin approached cityhood, Williams, Greene and Rome was ready to expand as well. Based on progressive factory architecture of the time, the four-storey Benton Street plant opened in 1913, boasting virtual glass walls, poured concrete construction, four-metre-high ceilings, and special safety features. In 1919, Williams, Greene and Rome was purchased by Cluett, Peabody and Company, and the trade name Arrow Shirts became the most recognized on the continent. (Courtesy KPL.)

Emil Vogelsang's button factory on Queen Street was part of a trend that earned Berlin the nickname "Buttonville." Vogelsang's partner, Jacob Y. Shantz, later ran his own concern that wound up on Water Street North as the Dominion Button Company. On June 9, 1909, a $150,000 fire destroyed the building, idling 150 workers. Superintendent David Gross bought the company, rebuilt on-site, and reopened in March 1910. Albert Snyder worked at Dominion and took this photograph of the reconstruction in November 1909. The firm closed in 1964, and the building was replaced by an apartment complex. (Courtesy WHS, Sokvitne.)

As the new Williams, Greene and Rome building went up, an even larger and more expensive structure arose to the west. The Consolidated Rubber Company (later Dominion Rubber) spent $1 million to erect architect Albert Kahn's design on Strange Street. Four storeys of poured concrete over a 150- by 30-metre plan would be a monumental undertaking today; imagine the difficulties overcome in 1912 by contractor Casper Braun. Large housing developments followed, more streets and services were added, and the west ward blossomed. Below, an aerial view from the 1950s shows the results. (Above, courtesy WHS; below, courtesy *Record*, UW.)

The third similar industrial building erected in early-20th-century Berlin was the Kaufman Rubber Company plant on King Street East at Victoria. Built in four phases between 1907 and 1925, Kaufman's is shown above, exaggerated with taste, in this early sketch. Like Dominion Rubber, the architect was Albert Kahn. A close-up of the inner courtyard area shows that details were not just for the facade. In the below photograph, a group of employees, including owner A.R. Kaufman (fourth from the left), pauses during a game of shinny. (Courtesy Kaufman Collection, UW.)

Kaufman Rubber produced many famous footwear brands during its nine decades—for example, Life-Buoy, Foamtreads, Sorel, and Funtreads. In the cutting room, linings, uppers, and soles were cut from patterned stock. Architect Kahn's use of glass walls shows to good advantage in this scene from a Kaufman publicity book. The family firm closed in 2000. (Courtesy Kaufman Collection, UW.)

Henry Nyberg arrived in 1913 with a plan to turn Berlin into an automobile manufacturing hub. He purchased much of Jacob Y. Shantz's old farm on the south side of King East in the Borden-Ottawa vicinity. His own Canadian Regal Motors kicked off the "auto boom," but when war came, Regal closed and Nyberg opened Dominion Truck. Four Wheel Drive of Wisconsin was producing sturdy, adaptable trucks when approached by Nyberg to set up in Berlin. By 1919, Four Wheel Drive trucks rolled off the line (see page 68). This one is destined for the Brant County Highways Department. (Courtesy Dave Moore.)

As might be expected in a community with substantial Germanic roots, brewing has long been a tradition. Although numerous private ventures operated around the village, the first significant effort came in 1840, when Farmers Inn owner Peter Rebscher started malting. He made the first Canadian lager and sold it for $4 a barrel. George Seip was the next brewer of note, starting his firm hopping in 1860 on Queen South. He closed in 1880. The longest-lasting brewery in Berlin began in 1898, when Christian Huether purchased land at King and Victoria. His Berlin Lion Brewery (above) was later known as Blue Top, Ranger, and simply Huether's. In 1952, Canadian Breweries Limited purchased the business and operated it as Dow Kingsbeer. Below, Kitchener photographer Roy Purkis was either lucky or patient in 1955 when he captured the juxtaposition of a Dow truck with a competitor's. (Above, courtesy WHS, *Berlin To-Day Reunion Souvenir,* 1906; below, courtesy WHS.)

Charles Andrew Ahrens built a three-storey shoe factory on Queen South in 1885, which now houses A Second Look Books. That building was sold to his son-in-law J.M. Schneider in 1908 because Ahrens wanted a larger, more efficient factory. He built it on Michael Street close to a Canadian Pacific Railway spur. This advertising card captures the bustle of the Michael Street site c. 1916. Charles Andrew Ahrens died in 1903, and his son Charles August took over. The firm was sold to Savage Shoes in 1949, but the building still stands, housing Music Plus. (Courtesy KPL.)

Berlin-Kitchener has always provided a healthy atmosphere for immigrant success. Walter Nowak arrived in 1913 from Poland and found work at both J.M. Schneider's and Dumarts, the two large meat packers. But Nowak chafed under others; he dreamed of his own business, and in 1933, opened Kitchener Packers on Spring Valley Road. Twenty-five years later, Walter Nowak and his sons Ted and Frank celebrate the growth and success of the family firm. Kitchener Packers closed in 1965, but the Nowak influence remains. Walter's grandson Mark was one of the founders of Kitchener's famous M & M Meats. (Courtesy Ted Nowak.)

Before hydroelectric power from Niagara Falls and before natural gas from the west, Berlin had electricity and lighting gas. Both came from the Gaukel Street plant shown above. As early as 1883, illuminating gas street lamps brightened the town. By 1887, the Berlin Gas Company was producing the town's electricity. Berlin purchased the private gas and electric company in 1903 for $90,000. The original plant had expanded greatly by the time the aerial photograph below was taken in 1919. The small gas holder site at the center left is now occupied by the Gaukel Street post office. The Charles Street bus terminal is currently located where the large gas holder in the centre stands. Directly above that gasometer is the building now housing Schreiter's Furniture. At the extreme left is McBrine Luggage. (Above, courtesy WHS; below, courtesy NAC.)

Five

Shop till You Drop

In 1880s Berlin, only one shopping mall had been built; it was located downtown on King Street with a few shops along side streets. Well-dressed men visited gent's furnishings establishments such as that of John Peters and Henry Hymmen on King Street East in the American Block. Young Louis Schwoob has been outfitted by the dapper Peters, and they both pose proudly. (Courtesy WHS.)

Shops, by their very nature, are elusive; they come and go, living only in old photographs. In 1925, Sippel Shoes at 31 King Street East closes. Of interest here is the "Denton & Gifford Photographers" sign in the window. Ernest Denton captured Berlin-Kitchener history for half a century. Many of his crisp, clear photographs are held in the archives, some appear in this book, but many more were lost in a mid-1950s fire in this very block. Downtowns traditionally offer opportunities to begin specialized businesses, but few evolve into long-running, well-known stores. To represent these "come-and-go" shops is the Kitchener Music and Novelty Store (below). Opening in 1941 at 157 King East, Anthony Gies offered gift, party, knick-knack, and entertainment items. The shop's location across from city hall and close to the out-of-town bus depot took advantage of the many service personnel stationed in Kitchener. (Above, photograph by Ernest Denton, courtesy KPL; below, courtesy Dave Moore.)

Individually owned food stores have virtually disappeared, but Busy Berlin boasted any number of family-operated grocery, fruit, meat, and bake shops. Over the next few pages, some of these fading-into-memory establishments return to the spotlight. Along Frederick Street, between King Street and the fire hall, a row of shops faced town hall and the market. In the mid-1880s photograph above, a proud L.F. Weber poses with his produce while a few gentlemen shoppers fill their baskets. The door behind leads up to the Berlin Suspender and Button Company, owned by Charles Hagedorn. Around this time, Jacob Shoemaker's store, located in the same block, sold a similar line. What appear to be double exposures in the below photograph are actually reflections in his shop window of the town hall, the market, and the Grand Central Hotel. (Courtesy KPL.)

M.J. Bailey Grocers is ready on this sunny morning in 1900; produce overflows onto the sidewalk, and the entire family gathers to serve. M.J. (right) and his wife, Clara (centre), have recently moved their business from Hamilton to 88 King West near Young. Their grandson Bill stands in the doorway. M.J. Bailey was a personable retailer. One story tells of how he painted a strangely shaped gourd to resemble a grotesque creature and then hid it in the apple barrel. Adams Tutti-Frutti gum is in the vending machine beside the doorway. (Courtesy WHS, Moffett.)

After one leaves King Street, a small grocery store appears at 62 Queen Street South. Snyder Brothers lasted only a couple of years, in existence c. 1908. In addition to groceries, the hanging signs remind passersby to pick up postage stamps and school supplies. The brothers were Albert and Joseph Snyder, great-grandsons of pioneer Joseph Schneider. (Courtesy WHS, Sokvitne.)

No. 62 was well stocked with Salada, Quaker, Tillson's, Kellogg's, Christie's, Polly, Jell-O, and other brand names. Tillie Massel prepares to serve while David Schneider, the owners' father, swaps a tale or two. In the photograph below, taken three years later, the products remain, but the proprietor has changed. Tillie Hunsberger's local merchandise includes Dietrich's bread and baked goods. Hunsberger's tenure did not last through World War I. Later occupants of No. 62 included Twin City Vulcanizing, General Battery, Predenchuk Fruits, Michael Forte, and Cookies That Care. Numbering changed in 1928, and 62 became today's 108, testimony to the ever-changing commercial streetscapes. (Above, courtesy WHS, Sokvitne; below, courtesy KPL.)

About four blocks north of King Street, Lancaster and Ellen cross Frederick at odd angles. The obvious nickname of the "Five Points" stuck with the site for almost 70 years. Henry J. Ahrens was the second son of Charles Andrew Ahrens (see page 47) but did not follow in his father's shoes. The 1903 photograph to the left shows Henry in front of his partially finished grocery store. Two years later, the Ahrens 5 Point Grocery a success, Henry and his wife, Caroline, welcome a customer. A small addition has been made for the associated 5 Point Meat Market. The Ahrens family owned the site until 1933, but several others operated the grocery business, including R.A. McDonald, Richard Kube, and Ernest Koehler. (Courtesy WHS.)

Above, the Ahrenses display a mélange of cereal, cigars, stuffed olives, candy apples, soaps, breads, and much more. In 1933, the store was rented by John Izma, a peripatetic fruit merchant. The Izmas eventually purchased the site and became so associated with the corner that the slightly altered phrase "Izma's Five Points" is still recognized by many. John's children, Bessie, Elizabeth, and Joe, made the grocery store into a neighbourhood institution until its closing in 1969. After the building was torn down, the resulting parkette was named Izma Green. Below, a late-1940s view captures the traffic enigma that was the Five Points. (Above, courtesy WHS; below, courtesy Steve Izma, *Record*.)

Where did Busy Berlin's vegetables and fruits come from? Some were purchased locally, but the exotics came by train to one of several wholesalers set up near the railyards. Grapes and peaches have just arrived, and the town's gentlemen grocers assemble to bid on the produce. This scene most likely takes place at the Longo Wholesale Market on Ahrens Street c. 1910. (Courtesy KPL.)

Weber Street West at College Street belonged to the Mansz family for more than 60 years. George Mansz started his butcher shop and meat market c. 1900, his special feature being home delivery via this trim pair of horses and wagons. The family operation lasted until the mid-1960s. (Courtesy WHS.)

Louis Bardon is typical of the 19th-century Berlin merchant. Born along the Rhine River in 1861, he learned baking before emigrating to Canada at age 22. Setting up a bakery on South Foundry Street (now Ontario), he combined hard work with a high product standard to build up a wide-ranging clientele. His wagons proudly proclaimed, "All Dough Mixed by Machine." Louis Bardon was active at St. Peter's Lutheran Church, was a member and president of the Concordia Society, and was a father of 10 children. After he died in 1917, his son Fred carried on until the late 1930s. In this 1890s photograph, Louis, displaying a wonderful mustache, is shown in the centre, surrounded by his sons and employees. Other early Berlin bakers included H.A. Dietrich and Mike Massel. (Courtesy WHS.)

Fresh milk came right to the customer's door, thanks to, from left to right, William Hopp, his son Oscar, and his employee Herschel Meyer. From 440 Lancaster Street West, Hopp's wagons provided one of the town's earliest home deliveries. Other dairies included Purity, Rosemount, Maple Lane, Rickert's, Westside, and Burkhardt. (Courtesy WHS.)

Giddup! Yoh! For youngsters, the daily clip-clop of the delivery wagons got more interesting as the sound became rarer. How does the horse know where to stop? Can I pet her? Can we have a ride? The disappearance of the horse from Kitchener streets is relieved periodically by the telltale sound of an Old Order Mennonite buggy. Dorothy Russell found the delivery man's appearance in 1924 noteworthy enough to capture Mr. Brubacher and his horse along David Street. (Courtesy Dorothy Russell.)

Richard Kube, after operating the 5 Point Grocery in the 1920s, was later to be found at his quaint booth on Queen Street South at Woodside Avenue. The Old Lantern boasted O'Keefe's Stone Ginger Beer, Silverwood's Instant Frozen Ice Cream, confections, and even light lunches. He served his neighbourhood as well as patrons of the nearby Woodside pool and sports field. The same booth was later moved to Highland Road and was operated by Adolph Aletter and Ralph Schwoob. (Courtesy VPHC, Dilys Miehm.)

Berlin-Kitchener markets have been an integral part of the community's shopping life since the 1840s. The town hall was built in 1869 with market vendors' stands in the basement. Participation grew rapidly, and a long, low structure was erected behind the town hall, as seen above. The weekly harvests of area farmers were brought in for the shopping pleasure of Berliners. This setup worked until 1906, when a clamour arose for a newer, larger facility. Beginning September 14, 1907, and open each Saturday for 65 years was a two-storey, red brick, 20- by 70-metre building fronting on Frederick Street. Generations of Berlin-Kitchener families took in the sights, smells, tastes, and temptations of locally produced farm goods. A bit of cheese, a few eggs, a quart of milk, and perhaps a jar of apple butter are all provided by the ladies below at a mid-1940s market. (Above, courtesy WHS; below, photograph by David L. Hunsberger, courtesy WHS.)

At the centre of Kitchener on April 24, 1953, the K-W Dutchmen Hockey Club paraded through the city with the Allan Cup (see page 99). Pilot Harvey Hall gently banked, allowing the camera a clear view of the city hall environs. At the right edge is the 1907 market building pointing to Duke Street and the block of shops across from the post office (see pages 65 and 66). To the left of city hall along Frederick is the short stretch of stores that housed the Shoemaker and Weber Groceries a half-century and more earlier (see page 51). Directly above the clock tower is the fire hall (see pages 67 and 68). Follow a line from the clock tower to the fire hall, and two blocks beyond, Tyson's white house appears (see page 22). Beside it is the Royal Canadian Legion (see page 32). At the left edge note the Fox Theatre sign; then follow King Street up to the first intersection and pick out the 1885 Benton Street post office (see page 65). (Courtesy WHS, *Record*.)

Six
SERVE US SERVICE

On one of the hottest days in the summer of 1923, a dozen men who had served as mayor gathered on a wooden platform, donned their widest-brimmed hats, and stared into the future through Ernest Denton's lens. The official cornerstone laying for Kitchener's long-awaited new city hall brought the former mayors together. As the Kitchener Musical Society Band played, the men lined up according to when they had served. Pictured here are, from left to right, the following: (front row) Dr. H.G. Lackner (1886–1887 and 1893), Louis J. Breithaupt (1888–1889), H.L. Janzen (1890), Daniel Hibner (1894–1895), John C. Breithaupt (1896–1897), and Charles Hahn (1909–1910); (back row) W.H. Schmalz (1911–1912), W.D. Euler (1913–1914), Dr. J.E. Hett (1915–1916), David Gross (1917–1919), Charles Greb (1921–1922), and current mayor L.O. Breithaupt, holding the silver trowel used to set the date stone. Carl Kranz (1904–1905) adjusts the stonework at the right. Two other former mayors, Aaron Bricker (1906–1907) and John R. Eden (1899–1900, 1902–1903, and 1920) attended but missed their camera date. (Courtesy WHS.)

Town hall began life in 1869 partly as a market with basement meat stalls, vendors' spaces, and a police lockup. The main floor was split between a post office and a council chamber. The second storey's large meeting and entertainment hall, complete with dressing rooms and a stage, became a community focal point. During its 54-year life, the council chamber (above) hosted village, town, and city municipal meetings. Pictured in 1903 are, from left to right, Police Chief George O'Neill, town clerk Edwin Huber, stenographer Alice Gauntley, market clerk Martin Huehnergard, and assistant treasurer Oswald Leyes. Town hall deteriorated and was unable to accommodate the new city's growing bureaucracy. Its replacement ready behind, the old building was demolished in September 1924, and again Ernest Denton captured the event (below). (Courtesy WHS.)

Several architects submitted sketches for the new city hall. Ironically, W.H.E. Schmalz's towerless plan (above) was chosen. His father, the 1912 mayor, had urged a replacement back then. When a clock tower was added, Toronto architect B.A. Jones was hired to modify the structure. That same clock tower was reconstructed 70 years later in Victoria Park. Kitchener City Hall immediately became the citizens' favourite and served, like its predecessor, for half a century. The early and rare view below, taken between 1924 and 1929, shows the wooden cross of remembrance, Kitchener's war memorial until the cenotaph was unveiled in 1929. (Above, courtesy WHS; below, courtesy Conrad Grebel College, UW, Joseph M. Snyder.)

It is the enduring image of a Kitchener Christmas. The 1945 holiday (above) must have been the sweetest Christmas of all, for the war was finally over. Something else made city hall special: the granite cenotaph (below). It took five years of suggestions, committees, fundraisers, and reports before Lt.-Gov. W.D. Ross unveiled the six-metre cenotaph on Victoria Day 1929. Ross invoked Rupert Brooke's "sweet wine of youth" lines to honour the fallen of World War I. For 20 years, the cenotaph stood on a traffic island at Frederick and King Streets. Finally, in 1949, it was relocated to what seems the obvious site, directly in front of city hall. When city hall was demolished, the memorial was moved to a garden beside the Duke Street post office, where Queen Elizabeth II reconsecrated it in 1973. (Above, courtesy *Record*; below, courtesy WHS.)

Just as imposing as city hall, the 1885 Benton Street post office connected this community to the world for 50 years. Before home delivery began in 1908, Berliners came downtown, stopped to chat a bit, and then picked up letters and parcels, postcards, and stamps. Between its closure in 1938 and its demolition in 1964, the building served as a recruitment centre, an armoury, and (above) headquarters for the 1954 centennial. One of Kitchener's few art deco buildings (below) opened in December 1938. A special feature was an observation gallery, allowing the postmaster to keep an eye on customers and workers. The building's stylish quality still attracts shutterbugs, as it did in the late 1930s, when Albert Fuller took this picture. (Courtesy WHS, Farrow.)

Not a public building as are others in this chapter, but one that merits note because of its proximity to them is this strip of shops built by W.H. Breithaupt in 1931. Stretching along Duke Street from Queen, almost to Frederick, the well-balanced block looks particularly pleasing without sign clutter. The first tenant was tailor Herman Ahrens (standing in the doorway). Other early shops included Freddie and Jack's Sporting Goods, Grip Tite Roofing, and the Sheehy Brothers. A bit later, Emma's Lunch, Karges Radio, Newtex Cleaners, and Harold Heer Photos set up shop. (Courtesy BHC, UW.)

Kitchener's second art deco public building within a year opened on June 26, 1939. Like the post office, it still stands, although all that the registry office now registers is applause for the theatrical presentations performed in the renovated interior. Much of the building's beauty remains—the colored-glass mosaic above the door, the stunning terrazzo floors, the fluted marble walls, and the wide-swinging doors. Dunker Construction built the $60,000 structure for the county of Waterloo and the cities of Galt and Kitchener. (Courtesy Dave Moore, published by Intaglio Gravure of Toronto.)

When Berlin was incorporated as a village in 1854, the council equipped a volunteer fire brigade based in a King Street blacksmith's shop, which became known as the "Spritzhaus." A somewhat better setup for fighting fires resulted in 1858, when the old Free Church was outfitted as a combination council chamber and fire hall, still staffed by volunteers. Finally, in 1874, a new fire hall was constructed, set back from the street, on Frederick between King and Duke. The wooden tower begged for a bell, and by 1877, a $700 beauty named Victoria was hoisted aloft. To the right is one of the few known photographs of the pre-bell fire hall. The same bell eventually wound up on top of city hall and was later situated in Victoria Park. Harry Guerin became fire chief in 1915 and served three decades, sometimes living in the tiny fire hall apartment shown below. He oversaw the transition from horses to trucks, from a small department to a multi-station force, and he instilled modern techniques in the firefighters. (Above, courtesy WHS; below, courtesy KPL.)

The 1922 Kitchener Fire Department (above) had a Chevy chief's car, a Ruggles hose truck, a Four Wheel Drive hose truck, and a Four Wheel Drive ladder truck. Chief Guerin (left) supervised two dozen professional firemen. Berlin-Kitchener has been fortunate in escaping those town-destroying fires that seemed to plague many Ontario communities. Of course, there have been many disastrous and sometimes fatal outbreaks. The December 16, 1959 fire (below) was one of the worst. In nine hours, flames devoured Zellers, Metropolitan, and Loblaws on King Street between Queen and Benton. Dozens of upper-storey offices, apartments, and firms were wiped out, resulting in damage of $1.5 million. No lives were lost, but a huge cultural loss was suffered when the entire sheet music collection, archives, instruments, and offices of the Kitchener Musical Society burned. Seventy-five years of music floated away as ash. This was just one of several late-1950s, early-1960s fires that transformed the downtown streetscape. (Above, courtesy KPL; below, courtesy *Record*, UW.)

68

Seven
GETTING AROUND

A car in every garage was a post–World War II phenomenon. Until then, how did people travel about? This single scene, c. 1910, illustrates the transition. On Factory Road (now West Avenue) at the creek, this photographer captured the past, the present, and the future. Four women and a boy loiter at the bridge. One has obviously ridden a horse. The others have walked (or used "shank's mare" in the vernacular). Up the hill in the background, one of those newfangled "auto-mo-biles" putters away, leaving its tire marks in the dust. (Courtesy WHS.)

A step up from walking and cheaper than a horse, bicycles caught on late in the 19th century. At least two bicycle-manufacturing firms set up in Berlin, and step-by-step with that came the growth of bike-repair shops. Just beyond the boys with the two-seater bicycle (and a pigeon-on-the-shoulder) is a sign for the General Repair Shop. Operated in 1925 by Gordon Braun and Cecil Wagner, it was the genesis of 2002's Braun's Bicycles, now in its third generation. Also noted on the sign is the name Shippling. Members of that family sometimes dropped the letter c, and today there is still a Schippling Bike Shop on Duke Street West. From this nondescript little repair shop of 1925, two 75-year-old businesses emerged. (Courtesy WHS.)

Automobiles began tootling down Berlin streets in the first decade of the 20th century, arousing interest, curiosity, and indignation. At first, car owners just stored gasoline at their homes, having picked it up at the hardware store. Soon, pumps invaded the streets of Berlin. Any merchant could install one at the curb. Early in the 1920s, Fred Berg provided Supertest gas outside his Vulcanizing Tire Repair business on King East near Cedar. Beside his shop, the bedding airs out on the balcony of the Germania Hotel. In 2001, when the city demolished a notorious east end hotel, wreckers and officials were surprised to find another building within, uncovering the old Germania. (Courtesy Harold Russell.)

College Street became the destination for local car owners who needed repairs of Ford products. In 1912, David and Nelson Gross boasted of running the most complete garage between Toronto and Winnipeg. O.W. Thompson took over the Gross business during World War I and hired a highly trained staff who, with their boss (left), posed outside 12 College Street. Note the company car, tow truck, and rather battered gasoline pump. After Thompson gave up the dealership in the late 1920s, the College Street site was vacated, and Hall and McKie built a new Ford dealership at King and Madison. The College location was demolished, and the Century Theater was erected. (Courtesy KPL.)

Wesley Wenzel was an early bird in the service station business. Remarkably, Wenzel's is still pumping gas. Located on King Street East, near Stirling, Wenzel's profited by being the last chance for gas in the city for those adventurous motorists heading south to Preston and beyond. In 1924, in what may have been the first local gas station stick-up, Wesley was threatened with a gun but managed to dash into the office. The thugs fled, and even the police department's "high speed car" could not catch up. Five years later, Wenzel's was flattened by a gas explosion; however, the business was rebuilt within a month and reopened, as seen here, for several more generations of service. (Courtesy KPL.)

As Kitchener grew, citizens demanded public transportation links to the King Street streetcars. The first substantial crosstown line began in January 1932, connecting St. Mary's Hospital to the Frederick Street city limits. Sanford Fischer and Charles Appell purchased and expanded this service, renaming it Kitchener Bus Lines. Over the next six years, they added drivers, routes, and buses. Kitchener's Public Utilities Commission purchased the business and began municipal service with new buses in May 1939. Passengers were happy to find their favourite Kitchener Bus Lines drivers had been hired by the commission. To the left, driver Art Stevens gases up a Kitchener Bus Lines bus in 1938 at the Duke Street Supertest station across from the post office. Below, former Kitchener Bus Lines drivers Sam Fischer (left) and Harold Appell, in their new Public Utilities Commission uniforms, stand beside one of the garish, red, canary yellow, and silver coaches. (Courtesy VPHC, Richard Appell.)

Streetcar service between Waterloo and Berlin began with horse-drawn cars in 1889 but was electrified in 1895. Two Breithaupt brothers, William H. and Ezra Carl, bought the street railway in 1896, including its branches to the train station and Bridgeport. By April 1907, the council purchased the operation and ran it under the Public Utilities Commission; however, the Bridgeport branch remained in Breithaupt hands. The King Street line soon extended to the eastern city limits near Rockway Gardens. New carbarns were erected in 1921 to house and repair the streetcars. At the same time, Kitchener Junction Station was built for passengers transferring to and from the inter-urban electric Grand River Railway. The barns, the station, and the Grand River Railway car are shown above in an early 1940s photograph by Paul H. Ziegler. When streetcars and automobiles met, it was a one-sided contest, as proven in the picture below from February 4, 1944, at the corner of King East and Dane Streets. Chester Madill attempted to turn into D.T. Brash's Supertest station (behind the streetcar). (Above, courtesy Laverne Hett; below, courtesy KPL.)

73

Two Grand Trunk freights collided in front of the Hibner Furniture factory near Duke Street. Some of Berlin's citizens are attracted by the activity, as crews try frantically to get the main line cleared. The accident scene is from an unidentified glass negative in the Waterloo Historical Society collection, and no other details have been uncovered. (Courtesy WHS.)

The gaiety for this gang of party boys will end quickly if the streetcar in the background catches up. What is the occasion? Why is the jigger bedecked with Union Jacks and strange ensigns? Who is this group heading out to Bridgeport? A good guess is that one of the younger Breithaupt boys, whose family operated the line, has borrowed the firm's jigger to take a birthday bunch out to Riverside for a day of celebrating (see page 108). (Courtesy WHS.)

King Street paving is disruptive now but was chaotic in 1910. The streetcar track was moved to a temporary bed on the south side. A cement railbed was poured wide enough to accommodate double tracking; bricks were then laid, one by one, on and around the railbed. The temporary tracks were removed and the roadway paved with bitumen. In the photograph above, King West businesses starting at Young Street, from left to right, are Edward Lippert Furniture, Peter Hymmen Hardware, Weber Chambers with the Singer Sewing Shop (columns), Waldschmidt Grocers, the Grand Union Hotel, a laneway, Stieler and Seibert Tailors, and the *Daily Telegraph*. Through the frost, traffic, streetcar vibrations, and asphalt-bubbling heat, the roads took a beating. In spring 1946, King Street was particularly damaged near the Waterloo border, as seen below. In one of the homes shown in the background, the boundary line runs through the living room; one year Waterloo got the taxes, the next year, Kitchener. (Above, courtesy Herb Ahrens; below, courtesy KPL, *Record*.)

Back when Grandpa walked barefoot uphill to school and snow fell every morning, just how were streets cleared? Take a dozen men, two horses, and a skid on runners. In this c. 1905 view from the American Hotel balcony, looking east, merchants have cleared the walk and now the "snow men" load the dray. Where the load was hauled and emptied remains unanswered. Clarke Brothers Drugs at No. 14 and Ritz Drugs at No. 26 are two of the north side shops. Some shovellers seem overly interested in a Beck and Schell's Grocery display. (Courtesy WHS.)

Bumpy roads inhabited Kitchener, even for those who took to the skies. Captain White, winner of the Distinguished Flying Cross, was an early aviation entrepreneur in the city. Using a grassy field near the Dominion Truck factory on Ottawa Street, he offered 20-minute flights and an air taxi service. One day in June 1919, as his motor failed, White attempted a landing in Henry Nyberg's orchard. No human injuries occurred, but the upper wing and motor suffered. At the scene were Joseph (surveying the damage) and Albert Snyder. Kitchener's east end was a cradle of local aviation; the area's first real airfield was located in the Sunnyside area in the mid-1920s. (Courtesy VPHC, Miriam Sokvitne.)

Eight
EVERY CITY HAS THEM

The institutions that backbone a community—medical, educational, and religious—are often seen as just structures, but the people using and staffing them, caught at odd moments, give life to the brick and steel memories. Opened officially on July 12, 1895, on land donated by Joseph Seagram, the Berlin and Waterloo Hospital operated privately until 1924, when the two communities assumed control. These nurses, on break c. 1905, maintain prim dignity while awaiting their own serving of hospital food. (Courtesy WHS.)

The original hospital structure was expanded several times before World War II. As the Twin Cities boomed after the war, facilities had to grow drastically to accommodate. A $4 million nine-storey addition was opened on May 25, 1951 (above). The crowd gathered around the new front door to watch Gov. Gen. Viscount Alexander of Tunis cut the ribbon. The aerial view (below), taken closer to 1960, shows that even the new structure soon grew, as excavation has begun for another wing. (Above, courtesy WHS, Farrow; below, courtesy KPL, *Record*.)

A corner lot at Church and Benton Streets held Berlin's first Methodist chapel and graveyard. By 1879, the vacated township hall on Queen North was renovated as the Trinity Methodist Church. Within 25 years, two old homes on Frederick Street were razed, and on August 14, 1905, the cornerstone of a new Trinity was laid. When Methodists, Congregationalists, and Presbyterians merged in 1925, Trinity became the dominant United church. (Courtesy KPL.)

Swedenborgians stretch back into Berlin's 1830s when Christian Enslin settled here. The budding congregation met at his house until constructing a shared Free church on Frederick Street. The Swedenborgians' next site was on the corner of Church and Benton Streets, where a church and graveyard were built. By 1870, one of the community's handsomest churches was erected at Water Street and King West. The Church of the New Jerusalem served for 60 years until the building and land were sold to the T. Eaton Company in 1929. The Swedenborgians' new Church of the Good Shepherd opened on Queen North in 1935. The Water Street church was then used by a Lutheran congregation until being replaced by an Eaton's store in 1950. (Courtesy WHS.)

Church Street bears only one church today, but, as seen previously, two others existed in the 1880s—and here is a third: St. Paul's Evangelical Lutheran. Two churches are shown above; the smaller Evangelical church faces Queen Street, while the steepled St. Paul's fronts on Church Street. The two were combined in 1889 in the still-standing structure, which is Kitchener's oldest church building. With such strong Germanic roots, it is no surprise that Berlin-Kitchener has had a dominant Lutheran base. Some 10,000 Lutherans attended the Quadra-centennial of the Reformation on September 3, 1917. All local Lutheran congregations, crossing synod lines, joined to organize a three-service program. One result is the best interior photograph of the Queen Street auditorium (below), captured, of course, by Ernest Denton. (Courtesy WHS.)

Church buildings do not a religion make, and some groups felt that only by externalizing their faith could they truly be faithful. Public baptisms are a tenet for several beliefs, and an untitled photograph in one of Viola Snyder's albums gives no hint of what congregation this is at the Bridgeport steel bridge. In any case, a good portion of this c. 1910 crowd is probably curious onlookers. (Courtesy WHS, Sokvitne.)

Sometimes public manifestations of faith got a little out of hand, and the public became annoyed. On Mill Street between Woodside Park, the railway tracks, and Highland Road was a large, old-growth bush (some of which remains today). For decades, its owners, Joseph Schneider's descendants, kept it as a camp meeting ground. Over a weekend, a week, or even a fortnight, a miniature village would spring up, and the faithful would come to testify. Mennonites and Pentecostals led the way in using the grounds. Preachers and some visitors lived under canvas; food was prepared and served in tents; first aid, sanitation, studying, and relaxing all took place in this tent town. During the Pentecostal meeting of June 26 to July 6, 1913, police were called by neighbours who testified themselves that they were fed up with the late-night noise and crowds. (Courtesy WHS.)

Roman Catholic schools and churches often marched hand-in-hand. The view above looks along Young Street to Weber, with the second St. Mary's Separate School in the foreground and the original St. Mary's Church behind. Berlin's first Catholic church, it was dedicated in 1856 and served until the current St. Mary's was constructed in 1903. Thereafter, the original building served as a community centre hosting dramatics, athletics, and dances until demolished in 1927. The school was built in 1874 but expanded several times before this c. 1900 photograph. The building was razed in 1965. The long history of St. Jerome's College stretches back to nearby St. Agatha in the 1860s, when Rev. Louis Funcken taught students advanced religious courses. Overcrowding caused an 1866 Berlin move to a house close to St. Mary's Church. In 1907, more than 100 priests who had trained under Funcken contributed to a bronze monument of the college's founder, shown to the left. The statue was made in Rome by Raffaele Zaccaquini and was erected within St. Jerome's landscaped campus. It has moved twice—in 1939 to the corner of Duke and Young and in the 1990s to the lawn of St. Mary's Church. (Above, courtesy KPL; below, courtesy Dave Moore, published by James MacCallum of Berlin.)

The 1856 Central School originally served as both a common (lower grades) and grammar (higher grades) school. Increasing numbers of students forced the grammar school to move on in 1872 (see page 85). After 1877, teachers-in-training attended model school classes at Central. Jeremiah Suddaby headed the school for 33 years, and upon his 1910 death it was renamed Suddaby. The 1899 model school class image above includes W.D. Euler (seated left) and librarian-author Mabel Dunham (seated fourth from left). Euler also appears in the 1897 staff photograph below (back row, left) when he was German-language instructor. Richard Reid (back row, right) was defeated by Mackenzie King in 1908. Suddaby (front row, left) oversaw many innovations, including Canada's first kindergarten in 1882 under Miss Metcalfe (middle row, third from left). The Central School still stands, part of the 1922 Suddaby School expansion. (Courtesy WHS.)

As Victoria looks down, only a few Central pupils manage a smile. On the blackboard, the 1890s timetable lists spelling, arithmetic, reading, writing, geography, literature, music, art, and hygiene. Leigh Hunt's poem "Abou Ben Adhem" is written out, making one wonder when Hunt was last taught in a public school. (Courtesy KPL.)

Berlin pioneered kindergarten in 1882, and it has been a regular feature ever since. These five-year-olds pose in front of Berlin's second public school, originally named Agnes Street but rebuilt and renamed King Edward. This 1925 class includes the following: (first row) Lloyd Shuttleworth (second from left) and Howard Underwood (sixth); (third row) Elaine Warren (far left) and Hilda Berg (far right); (fourth row) Harold Kreiner (second), Carl Slumski (fifth), Bob Mills (sixth), and Ken Helm (eighth). (Photograph by Denton; courtesy Bob Mills.)

Joining Central and Agnes Street, in 1890, Berlin's third public school, Courtland Avenue, was opened. Miss M. Hyndman was sub-principal, and within three years, Courtland had also accepted kindergarten pupils. Although the original structure had an attractive front, Joseph Snyder chose to photograph the rear in May 1916. The large steel tower at the right is the St. George Street water stand. Courtland, like all the early schools, has changed by being either rebuilt or built around. (Courtesy WHS, Sokvitne.)

Increasing enrollment forced the grammar school to leave Central in 1872. For three years, classes were taught in the vacant Swedenborgian building on Church Street. As 1876 dawned, a new $5,800 high school opened at Greenbush, the height of land between Berlin and Waterloo. School trustees hired Galt's David Forsyth as a teacher under principal James Connor. These two oversaw the education of area teenagers for almost half a century. Connor was succeeded as principal by Forsyth, who then served from 1901 to 1921 (see page 94). In 1899, the high school was given a $6,000 remodelling, and shortly afterwards, this snowy scene captured that hallowed hall of higher learning. (Courtesy WHS, Sokvitne.)

Apart from a place of learning, the Kitchener Collegiate Institute has been an important community centre. Its large auditorium has hosted numerous public events such as this December 1947 combined concert by the Kitchener Musical Society Band and the institute's girls chorus. (Courtesy Laverne Hett.)

The Kitchener Collegiate Institute's spring 1929 operetta, *Rings in the Sawdust*, told the age-old tale of the banker's daughter (Helen Shantz) falling in love with the visiting circus manager (Douglas Brown). This photograph was donated to the Waterloo Historical Society by another of the institute's fondly recalled, long-serving teachers, F.W.R. Dickson, who guided students through many productions. (Courtesy WHS.)

Nine
Having Fun

The student performances on the previous page reveal one of the many ways in which Berlin-Kitchener residents have entertained themselves. Sports, music, movies, parks, and camping are all in the spotlight. Moving pictures came to Berlin in the mid-1890s, and before World War I, movie houses had opened in various downtown locations. One man's name runs through the Berlin movie story: George "Pop" Philip. It was Pop who welcomed Berliners to the first movie houses in town. Here, Pop (pictured here in a grey coat) welcomes a group of travelling actors to the first Star Theatre, which he operated from 1907 to 1910 at 15 King West (the Walter Ziegler sign in the photograph is in error). (Courtesy WHS.)

As he ran the first Star Theatre, Pop also showed motion pictures at the Theatorium on the north side of King West, where Theatre and Company is now located. The Theatorium's sign boasted its 5¢ admission and is visible in this 1910 King Street paving scene (see page 75). Pop had previously managed the Clarendon Hotel (right, later site of Goudies). Between the Clarendon and the Theatorium were buildings housing Wanless Pianos, Paul Pequegnat Jewellers, and Alex Rose Ladies' Wear. (Courtesy WHS.)

The Longo family ran fruit stores at several Berlin and Waterloo locations, and for a while Leo Longo was also a motion picture entrepreneur. Beside his King and College fruit store, he opened the Roma Theatre in 1914. Al Beckerich was an early manager of the Roma, transforming it into the most attended theatre in the city. The Roma later operated as the Imperial and the New Princess before closing its doors in 1925. This 1916 Denton photograph details the Roma's entrance when *Gloria's Romance*, starring Billie Burke, was the main attraction. (Courtesy Dave Moore.)

A crisp 1914 Denton photograph illuminates a Berlin theatre's interior. Unfortunately, the theatre is unidentified. The matte is signed by Al Beckerich to Henry Janzen "from his old manager." Beckerich managed the Roma, and Janzen built the Grand, but Beckerich also ran the Grand for a short while. Is this the Roma or possibly the Grand? Judging by the heavy coats, the heating was surely on the fritz. (Courtesy KPL.)

Henry Janzen's Grand Theatre was located on King West near Gaukel. Manager Beckerich appears in the middle of this photograph, with his hat pushed back, welcoming the vaudeville company described on the posters—Shepard and Edwards, Demonde Densmore and Dixie, and Volta the Electrical Wizard. For such engagements, the Grand became the Grand Opera House. In this January 1915 scene, upcoming movies include *The Outlaw* and *A Modern Jekyll and Hyde*. The Allen Theater chain purchased the Grand in April 1918 and changed the name to the Allen. By late summer 1922, with two new modern movie palaces, the Capitol and the Lyric, attracting all the business, the Allen closed and Janzen remodelled the site into shops. An early tenant was Budd Clothing, still operating. (Courtesy WHS.)

Movie houses and vaudeville theatres brought in famous outside performers, but Berlin had significant home-grown artists. This turn-of-the-century studio photograph contains one of the great "what-ifs" of Berlin history. The caption reads, "Sextette from Floradora," and shows a dozen costumed performers. *Floradora* was one of the favourite light musical pieces of the era. The list of Berlin singers is incomplete. The women are, from left to right, Mary Lackner, Emma Davison Richmond, Daisy Hilborn, Blanche Clement, Martha Stewart, and Fannie Brown. Only three men's names are given: Shannon Bowlby, Carlo Boehmer, and Dr. Ruddell. Boehmer jumps out of the photograph; he is second from right. Born and raised in Berlin, Charles Henry Boehmer was a star goalie for Berlin's first-ever championship hockey team in 1897 and served on early hockey executives. But Boehmer also had a voice, and what a voice it was! He dropped his sports connections and university studies to devote his life to becoming a great tenor. Boehmer and Guelph's Edward Johnson (later manager of the Metropolitan Opera) were friends for years and studied together in New York. Singing to great applause in the United States was not enough for Boehmer; he took up further studies with the great voice maestros of Milan, Italy. There he befriended such legends as Enrico Caruso and John McCormack. Using the stage name Carlo Nardi, Boehmer attracted the attention and devotion of the sternest critics the Italian press could muster. Then came the outbreak of World War I and the disarray of the Italian music scene. Boehmer sailed to New York and returned to Berlin to work with his family's Boehmer Box Company. Although he sang locally in a few patriotic concerts, by the time war had ended, business pressures and a diminished musical passion ended his operatic aspirations. The possibilities are fascinating. What if World War I had not broken out? Would he have fulfilled the predictions of so many musical experts? Would he have been the next Caruso? Before his death in 1962, Carlo Boehmer had much time to ponder the possibilities. (Courtesy KPL.)

The Kitchener-Waterloo Philharmonic Choir was a 1922 reincarnation of earlier Berlin choirs. From the beginning it was blessed with directors of rare talent, including Harry Hill, Glenn Kruspe (centre, with baton), Frederick Pohl, Don Landry, and Howard Dyck. Miss Ada Eby sits at the piano, as she did for almost 30 years. Behind Kruspe and two to the left is a face that later became one of Kitchener's best known, Elaine Cole of CKCO-TV. During the war, Kruspe organized an instrumental ensemble, and from this grew today's respected Kitchener-Waterloo Symphony. (Courtesy KPL.)

Music satisfies many aspects of the human psyche—intellectual, emotional, martial, and more. In the midst of the 1915–1916 upheavals, the Berlin Musical Society Band was highly visible in its military role as the Band of the 108th Regiment. Seen here in April 1916, the band leads the locally raised overseas battalion, the 118th, down Queen Street South towards King. At the right is the facade of the Walper Hotel. Just past the Dominion Café sign is the awning-covered entrance to the second Star Theatre. (Courtesy Margaret Farrow.)

Across the country, concert bands fine-tuned for the annual competitions at the Canadian National Exhibition (CNE). No one kept his band in better training than Kitchener Musical Society conductor George Ziegler. For well over three decades under his leadership, the band entered and won numerous competitions. In this 1951 photograph by Mel Riepert, Ziegler puts the Kitchener Musical Society Band through its paces at the CNE's distinctive main bandshell. (Courtesy Laverne Hett.)

In addition to his work with the Kitchener Musical Society Band, Ziegler also operated the Kitchener Conservatory of Music. Under the society's umbrella, he organized, trained, and led the famous ladies' band, a boys' band, a junior boys' band, and in 1952, a combined boys' and girls' band. The young musicians of the latter prepare to practice at the Kitchener Musical Society hall. Located on King East between Queen and Benton, the hall was later destroyed by fire (see page 68). Standing at the rear are Harold Ballantyne (left) and George Ziegler (right). (Courtesy Laverne Hett.)

In tribute to its fallen men and women, Kitchener erected the state-of-the-art Kitchener Memorial Auditorium on East Avenue. At the official opening in fall 1951 (above), the Kitchener Musical Society Band became the first to make music within the auditorium. What makes this scene unique is George VI's portrait. He died in early 1952, so his huge photograph was not on display very long. The big beat came to Kitchener in August 1956 (below), when a rock-and-roll dance was booked. Featuring the Cadets, Big Joe Turner, and the Choker Campbell Orchestra, the event was watched by a bemused Sandy Baird, the *Record*'s clever quipster. "The jiving couples, as always, danced like they were barefooted on a hot sidewalk and trying to back away but couldn't get their hands unstuck." Nine hundred fans attended, and a second concert was booked for September. Auditorium manager Bob Crosby promised free admission to any parent accompanying a teenager. (Above, courtesy Laverne Hett, *Record*; below, courtesy *Record*.)

In Colin Jose's *Keeping Score: The History of Canadian Soccer*, the reader reaches only page 3 before David Forsyth's name appears. He truly was the father of soccer in southern Ontario. Coinciding with his involvement in sports were Forsyth's contributions to secondary education in Berlin-Kitchener. Born in Scotland in 1852 but arriving as an infant in Canada, Forsyth came to Berlin in 1876 after graduation from the University of Toronto. As master of mathematics and science at Berlin High School, he teamed with principal J.W. Connor and master Adolph Mueller to give area students outstanding instruction and guidance (see page 85). In the first year, he formed a team called the Berlin High Schools, which did not play against other schools but was a town club on which he and other non-students played, challenged, and beat other Ontario teams. The High Schools later became the Rangers, who, in the blue and white uniforms, brought back many championships. Forsyth was also instrumental in forming several Ontario soccer leagues and helping to administer them. He captained all-star Canadian clubs that toured Britain and the United States. Other sports also attracted Forsyth; he became captain of Berlin's lacrosse team and also was a cricket player, a proficient lawn bowler, a famed bicyclist, and (as seen on page 2) an indomitable canoeist. As a member of the Waterloo Historical Society, he donated this photograph, which shows the final gathering of the High Schools club. In 1884, the club adopted the Rangers name, likely patterned after his native Scotland's Glasgow Rangers. Posing with the championship trophy of the Western Football Association are, from left to right, the following: (front row) Herb Bowlby, David Forsyth, Ed Rife, Adolph Mueller, and Harv Bingham; (back row) Fred Bowman, Joe Brubacher, Tom Gibson, Jack Dolph, Theodore Hughes, and Tom Sheppard. The Berlin High Schools soccer team was the community's first championship club in any sport. (Courtesy WHS.)

Like soccer, Berlin's curling history involves a Scottish connection. The vagaries of outdoor curling annoyed a group of Scottish-Canadian Berliners, so they built the town's first indoor ice rink in 1883. A frame structure near Gaukel Street and Hall's Lane, it featured natural ice. Skating and hockey were also based in that near-forgotten rink. The Granite Club on Agnes Street was built in 1927 with five sheets of natural ice, but an artificial ice plant was soon installed. For a few years, public skating and winter carnivals shared ice time with the curlers. This 1951 trophy-winning Granite rink is just one of many such champions. (Courtesy WHS.)

Of the major team sports, lacrosse has had the lowest profile, but there has always been a small group of dedicated enthusiasts. Kitchener-Waterloo's 1930 club gathered in Victoria Park with manager Andrew Eaton (kneeling, second from the right). (Courtesy Jack Eaton.)

Golf began catching on with Berliners in the first decade of the 20th century, and its popularity has never waned. In fall 1909, a group organized the Grand River Golf and Country Club and built a nine-hole course between Bridgeport and the sugar factory. It was a members-only club until 1931, when a Toronto concern purchased the course and clubhouse, setting green fees at 50¢ and charging double on weekends. Bill Bailey (right) and his friend come to the fore in the early 1930s at the Grand River course. (Courtesy WHS, Moffett.)

The Grand River Club was sold because a number of its members had constructed a new golf course. Eighteen holes were laid out on land straddling the boundary of Kitchener and Waterloo. With its expensive membership fee, Westmount quickly became the place to be for the area's business and professional elite. An early view of the Westmount clubhouse survives through the photographs of John Steven Carroll. His Bank of Montreal career touched the Twin Cities for a brief time in the 1930s, and his ever-present camera preserved numerous Depression-era sights. In August 1932, he visited Westmount. (Courtesy WHS.)

Visitors to Kitchener are sometimes puzzled by the still common expression "sewer farm." The town's earliest attempt at processing sewage began in 1891, when a farm was purchased on Mill Street beside Schneider Creek. Filtration beds and pipes were laid down, the clear water effluent drained into the creek, and the remaining material built up and turned into vegetable fields. Alterations over the years expanded the farm from Mill Street towards King. By the early 1930s, the sewer farm was unable to keep up with Kitchener's growth, so a $500,000 plant was built at Doon beside the Grand River. The old site was debated at council, and a lobby urging a city-run golf course won. Using relief workers, the old sewer farm was landscaped into a rolling 18-hole course. Close to King Street, one of the city's jewels, Rockway Gardens was developed, featuring colorful flowerbeds, goldfish ponds, fountains, and attractive shrubbery. The heart of any golf course is its clubhouse, and this is Rockway's early version, where champions such as Gary Cowan, Gerry Kesselring, and Moe Norman launched their careers. (Author's collection, published by Intaglio Gravure of Toronto.)

Perfectly trimmed grass is important not only to golfers; for lawn bowlers, it is of prime concern. Lawn bowling stretches back to 1890s Berlin. The still-operating Kitchener Lawn Bowling Club traces its roots to 1902. Among the early members were Dr. G.H. Bowlby, David Forsyth, and a famous quartet who won the 1909 Ontario championship, consisting of W.D. Euler, W.G. Cleghorn, Herman Boehmer, and Harvey Sims. Amazingly, three of them—Cleghorn, Sims, and Euler—participated in the British Empire Games 25 years later. Until 1962, the bowling green was located behind the county jail between Queen and Frederick. Some 1912 activity is captured in this photograph by W.G. Cleghorn. (Courtesy WHS, Farrow.)

The history of hockey in Berlin-Kitchener fills an entire book by itself. From the early days on the Shantz millpond to the 1883 Gaukel ice barn, and from the 1904 Queen Street rink to the 1951 Kitchener Memorial Auditorium, young men have developed their skills and filled professional hockey's ranks. What a team the Twin Cities could have put on the ice in the late 1930s! Many great local players of that era did play on one team, but in a different sport: Carling Kuntz Brewery sponsored an exhibition ball team. With their club affiliations attached, here is the all-star lineup. They are, from left to right, as follows: (front row) mascot Billy Hainsworth (son of George Hainsworth); (middle row) Honey Kuntz (Kitchener Seniors), Bobby Bauer (Boston Bruins), manager George Hainsworth (retired NHL star with the Montreal Canadiens), Gene Bauer (Kitchener Seniors), and Howard Mackie (Hershey Bears); (back row) Milt Schmidt (Boston Bruins), Ott Heller (New York Rangers), Woody Dumart (Boston Bruins), Morris Gerth (English League), Dick Behling (Detroit Red Wings), Vic Lang (Kitchener Seniors), and Red Keating (Detroit Red Wings). Schmidt, Bauer, and Dumart joined the Boston Bruins in 1937 and achieved fame as the "Kraut Line" primarily over the next four seasons, and their great skills are revered by longtime Boston fans. Heller had a lengthy Ranger career and won Stanley Cups with them in 1933 and 1940. (Courtesy WHS.)

98

Mid-century hockey revolved around the Kitchener-Waterloo Dutchmen senior team. Playing out of the ultra-modern auditorium made the club reach a bit higher. A 5-0 May 6, 1953 win over Penticton set off a still-remembered celebration of the city's first Allan Cup since 1918. Fireworks, streamers, car horns, and screaming fans made the downtown into a late-night carnival. An impromptu parade (above) wound from the auditorium to city hall, letting the Dutchies bask in the fans' cheers. Two years later, with many of the same players, the Dutchmen repeated. As 1955 Allan Cup champions, they also won the right to represent Canada at the 1956 Olympics in Cortina, Italy. Special envelopes and stamps (below) helped publicize the Olympic appearance. In an era when gold seemed a Canadian birthright, the club's bronze disappointed many. It, however, did not deter 20,000-plus Twin Cities fans from attending the welcome-back parade on February 10, 1956 (below). In the crowd was Albert Schmid of Germany, who lived here briefly in the 1950s. Following his death many years later, his family in Germany donated his Kitchener photographs. (Above, courtesy Murray Fried; both below, courtesy KPL.)

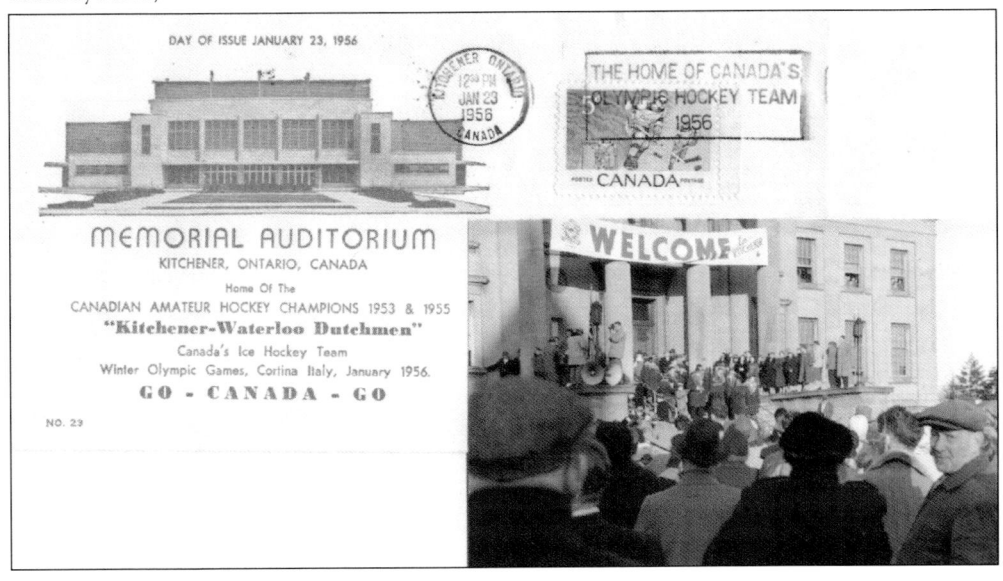

Hockey, like other sports, has value far beyond the livelihood and excitement it provides at the professional level. For every Hall of Famer, thousands more play just for fun. These thousands learned on frozen backyards or on Victoria Park Lake and often played for company-sponsored teams on rinks beside the plant (see page 44). Sports fostered camaraderie and loyalty amongst workers. Arrow Shirts, as noted, had an active employee welfare program; by the mid-1930s, 375 out of 400 workers took part in one Arrow Club sport or another. On Arrow's future Benton Street parking lot, a large rink (above) welcomed players from the company and the neighbourhood. More organized was the 1943 Arrow Club basketball team (below), which won the city's industrial league trophy. Fifth from the left is Dorothy Gress. (Above, courtesy KPL, Arrow; below, courtesy Lori Mills.)

Skating carnivals began outdoors in Victoria Park in the early 1920s. By the late 1930s, the Kitchener-Waterloo Skating Club's presentations combined local and professional talent at the Queen Street auditorium. Camera buff Leonard Bidwell devoted most of his spare time to photography. His albums are full of technical details, and his photographs capture two decades of Kitchener life. This synchronized skating shot was taken during the 1939 Skating Carnival at the Queen Street auditorium. (Courtesy WHS, Marg Leiher.)

Until the 1960s, there was that one special day when classes from every school in the city marched to Victoria Park for Field Day. The 50-yard dash, the javelin, the running broad jump, and the shot put were among those exotic sports offering their prize ribbons. This 1947 23rd Annual Field Day winner's quartet featured, from left to right, Bob Rieck, high jump; Donna Bricker, girls' short potato race; Elmer Hintz, senior hop, step, and jump; and Douglas Hartman, senior hurdles. The proudly worn ribbons were pinned on by special judges Milt Schmidt, Syl Apps, Dutch Hiller, and Woody Dumart, all NHL idols. (Courtesy WHS, *Record*.)

101

Baseball had built up a coterie of fans in Berlin by 1890. Most play took place within the city until the Inter-County League was formed after World War I. The 1914 Berlin Cubs featured future NHL star George Hainsworth, and the team's only pitcher was Allen Shirk. (Courtesy WHS.)

The names scrawled on the back of this mid-1920s Forsyth softball team photograph (although many of them are misspelled) are Anette Arche, Louis Steffler, Hazel Walper, Clarina Kuntzie, Alice Klem, Esther Sengbusch, Katherine Schmitt, Erma Sengbusch, Olive Sengbusch, Mable Snyder, Sahra Keller, Bill Sengbusch, and Redge Dausett. The picture was taken at Victoria Park. Forsyth Shirts, like Arrow, had a vibrant employee recreation association and sponsored clubs in several city sports leagues. (Courtesy KPL.)

Victoria Park's role in athletics, recreation, entertainment, and civic events is hard to overestimate. Since its mid-1890s development on the final remnants of Joseph Schneider's original land, the park hosted every type of community activity. In winter, the lake's frozen surface was a mecca for toddlers, teens, courting couples, cruising singles, hockey players, and slower-paced seniors. Leonard Bidwell stood along David Street on a sunny, frosty day in February 1939 to preserve a classic Kitchener image. (Courtesy WHS, Marg Leiher.)

An ice storm always brings out the shutterbugs, and with the variety of trees in Victoria Park, the resultant icy images bend every which way. In this view dated February 22, 1922, an unidentified photographer's lens focuses on the park's new pergola. This shelter was one of three built that year, two of which still serve park visitors. Today, Victoria Park centres a neighbourhood heritage district; even development within the park must conform to historic themes and vistas. (Courtesy VPHC, Dona Paul Massel.)

The original pavilion in Victoria Park (above) was actually designed as a picnic shelter. Architect Charles Knechtel's turretted folly became an immediate favourite for newcomers and residents. In addition to sheltering thousands of weekend picnickers when it rained, it also housed a restaurant, hosted dances, welcomed special city visitors, and provided a wonderful view from its topmost turret. It was burned down in March 1916 as a result of the troubled times in wartime Berlin. Grand opening day for Victoria Park was August 27, 1896, with a huge celebration featuring fireworks, athletics, music, bike races, prizes, and baseball. When photographer A.S. Green took a series of opening-day pictures, he caught part of Berlin's first-ever, and rather meagre, regatta (below). (Above, courtesy WHS; below, courtesy VPHC.)

Victoria Park has always been a focus for family activities such as picnics, weddings, birthdays, reunions, and other celebrations. Relatives and guests from out of town were taken to the park for relaxing strolls and light lunches beside the lake. When Berlin officially became a city in 1912, the Ahrens clan gathered for a picnic with cousins, aunts, and uncles. At the park's first playground swings, Herman Ahrens, son of Charles Andrew Ahrens and brother of Henry J., stands in a suit with his hands at his sides. The whole family is dressed up, which, considering that Herman was a tailor, is not too surprising. Another brother holds the Berlin cityhood pennant. (Courtesy VPHC, Herb Ahrens.)

Berlin was a long way from the Grand River, but citizens always enjoyed its waters. Near Breslau at the Kolb farm, Dorothy White (left) and her aunt Florence Schantz (third from the left) escape the city's heat in that last golden summer before war erupted in August 1914. (Courtesy Dorothy White Russell.)

Bridgeport was often called Berlin's recreation suburb. Campgrounds were developed along the shoreline, and many companies booked annual picnics. These young women from Williams, Greene and Rome did not lack a date for the big day. (Courtesy WHS, Sokvitne.)

Downstream from Bridgeport where there was a bit more privacy, family camps and cottages were built under the western bluffs. Albert Snyder and his family spent several summers here under canvas. He invited some Dominion Button Company co-workers to enjoy a day at the river c. 1911. His daughter Viola wears the dark dress. (Courtesy WHS, Sokvitne.)

Albert Snyder's family and friends created a shady, cozy canvas corner in the woods beside the river, including deck chairs, a mirror nailed to a tree, and an enamel washbasin, all items indicative of a 1910 "roughing it" experience. In the evening, all the campers gathered around a huge bonfire at the river's edge to swap stories and enjoy sing-alongs. Other families camping in the area were the Oscar Boehmers, the Charles Simpsons, and the M.E. Shantzes. (Courtesy WHS, Sokvitne.)

Down the river a little more, the campgrounds gave way to more substantial summer homes. The Breithaupt family cottage, Riverbend, was one of several built under the embankment. Mounted on sturdy tree trunks to withstand spring floods and ice floes, the cottage gave the Breithaupts a cool, nearby summer retreat to entertain large groups of friends and to escape Busy Berlin's heat. (Courtesy BHC, UW.)

W.H. Breithaupt ran the Berlin and Bridgeport Electric Street Railway and developed the impressive 1903 pavilion as the centrepiece of his Riverside Park in Bridgeport. It had a kitchen, dining hall, change rooms, lockers, dance floor, covered verandah, bowling alleys, and a grand view of the riverscape. A surrounding park with bandstand and sports fields provided lots of room for fun-filled visits. Broad stairs led down the 16-metre embankment. There, a cable ferry took picnickers across the river to another park, which had been built by Bridgeport's citizens for camping, fishing, and picnics. The pavilion soon became known as the Casino and hosted conventions, reunions, holiday celebrations, and school picnics. This church group of mostly young people (above) enjoys sandwiches and snacks on the verandah in 1916; it includes Dorothy White (left) and Viola Snyder (right). The river and steel bridge provide a backdrop in 1913 as Bill Bailey (below, inset) balances on the edge of the verandah. Seen from across the river, the pavilion's dramatic perch and wooden picket fence attract the eye. (Above, courtesy Dorothy Russell; below, courtesy WHS; below inset, courtesy WHS, Moffett.)

Ten
BATTLE LINES

The outbreak of World War I in August 1914 terminated the Busy Berlin era of prosperity, growth, harmony, and happiness. As the war dragged on and reports of death and injury filled the newspapers, feelings throughout Canada hardened against the enemies—Germany and Austria. In Berlin, Ontario, the presence of so many people of Germanic background, as well as the city's name, provided an ideal target for propagandists and hatemongers. Post-war studies have shown that enthusiasm for the war in Berlin was consistent with comparable cities. Young men, such as Wilbert "Bill" Bailey (left) joined the local battalion. Many more entered service through other area units or enrolled in specialized regiments in Toronto. A bit of leave in Victoria Park gave Bill and his pals a chance to pose for the camera in May 1916. (Courtesy WHS, Moffett.)

In addition to young Canadians eager to join, many others had military responsibilities. First, some Germans and Austrians held commissions in their native countries' armies. Early in the war, they were granted special identification cards after swearing they would not attempt to leave Canada or commit espionage. Second, many British reservists lived across Canada; they were mobilized and sped eastward to catch ships for England. Four Berlin residents with previous British service said goodbye on August 18, 1914. Being sent off by a uniformed cavalry reservist are, from left to right, Pvt. A.E. Ryder, Sgt. A.H. Davis, Pvt. H. Aylward, and Pvt. A. Morton. (Courtesy KPL.)

Berlin had only a small militia unit at the outbreak of the war. Young men wanting overseas duties enlisted in other area battalions such as the 71st and 34th. In Guelph, where the 34th was based, B Company, seen here in the armoury, consisted entirely of Berlin men. Some 75 of them transferred to the new North Waterloo 118th Battalion in late 1915. (Courtesy KPL.)

110

On September 17, 1915, at the invitation of W.G. Weichel, MP, the Canadian minister of militia, Sir Sam Hughes, visited Berlin. Weichel's welcome included, "I, of German descent . . . have no reason to be otherwise than proud of it." Hughes's reply was, "This is not a struggle against the German people . . . but against Prussian autocracy and despotism." One year later, both expressions would have been impossible. A huge patriotic rally gave a hero's welcome to Berliners serving with the 34th and 71st who had been given leave to attend. Hughes's speech ended with a prediction that in 12 months, many Berlin, Ontario boys would march with him into Berlin, Germany, triumphant. Ernest Denton's detailed photograph captures the 108th Militia Battalion lining up for inspection. Col. H.J. Bowman (with the swagger stick) and General Hughes have just reached the final soldier in the line. (Courtesy KPL.)

Two months later, Hughes authorized raising local men for the 118th Battalion. The 118th has received much blame for the subsequent months of Berlin's agony. However, it is important to remember that the battalion consisted of a number of young men and inexperienced officers led by senior officers with little military command experience. The 118th was a familiar sight in Berlin from its November 1915 formation until its May 1916 departure for London, Ontario's Camp Carling training grounds. On a chilly spring day in 1916, somewhere on Berlin's outskirts, a company of 118th soldiers is at ease during a route march. (Photograph by Aaron Kolb; courtesy WHS.)

Among those in the previous photograph may have been Sgt. Wilbert "Bill" Bailey, who has appeared previously in this book. The 22-year-old appears in the middle of the front row as a 118th parade pauses on King Street (left). Bailey returned from overseas, raised a family, and was a prominent member of the Royal Canadian Legion in Kitchener. These other two men did not return alive. Pvt. Alexander Ralph Eby (below, left) was the first native of Berlin killed in the war. He was also, ironically, a direct male descendant of one of Berlin's founders, Bishop Benjamin Eby. Twenty-year-old Harold Voelker (below, right) joined the 118th in 1916. At 21, he was wounded at Passchendaele. Harold Voelker did, in a fashion, come home. His wounds resulted in such full paralysis that the remainder of his short life was spent confined to Toronto's Euclid Hall hospital. A full military funeral was held at Kitchener's Mount Hope Cemetery on December 5, 1920. Harold Voelker is possibly the sole Berlin boy to return home only in death. Officially, no overseas fatalities were returned to Canada (except for the Unknown Soldier in Ottawa; most injured soldiers were able to visit their families at least once). Alexander Ralph Eby and Harold Voelker are just two of 90 Berlin boys who perished. (Above, courtesy WHS, Moffett; both below, courtesy KPL.)

Photographs in the early years of the century could be printed as postcards. This fad has meant that many intimate snapshots have survived. Two local cards give us candid peeks at life in the 118th Battalion. George Schneider of Victoria Street South and J. Schultz were pals in the 118th. The mess tent photograph was sent by Schultz (above, extreme left) to George's sister Lena from Camp Borden sometime in the summer of 1916. Did they ever meet again? George went overseas with the 118th, but no J. Schultz is listed on the 118th muster. Half of its members were "washed out" as medically unfit on the eve of the battalion's departure for England in January 1917. Much less is known of the sextet below. It is another postcard but was unmailed. Each man wears a cap with the 118th badge, and two wear homemade 118th sweaters. (Courtesy Bob Vogel.)

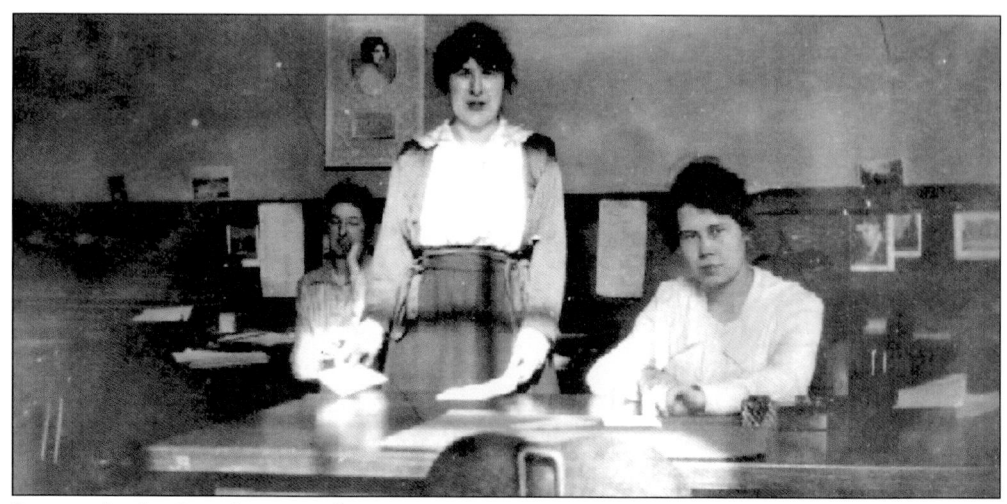

Support for the Canadian war effort went on in many ways at home. Businesses manufactured war goods; for some, this meant producing the same product (for example, Arrow Shirts just made more shirts), while others switched to primary military items (Buffalo Forge on Highland Road turned out artillery shells). Volunteers worked behind-the-scenes more than ever. Expanding its normal duties, the Red Cross Society organized an efficient wartime organization. Thousands of items were sent overseas to soldiers, military hospitals, and refugee camps—everything from pillowslips and knitted face cloths to abdominal binders and scarves. Under president Agnes Jackson, hundreds of volunteers toiled long hours to keep the supplies flowing. Ethel Lapsley and Edith Ahrens, seen here in January 1918, were two of the Red Cross workers. They remained lifelong friends and married within a week of each other in 1925, Ethel to Norman Schneider and Edith to Hy MacDonald, founder of MacDonald Electric. Ethel served the Red Cross for 60 years, beginning with her knitting work in World War I. (Courtesy Betty and Herb Schneider.)

A soldier's battle often did not end with the return home. Many suffered from barely understood mental stresses and scars. Even before the war ended, Kitchener had a chapter of the Great War Veterans' Association. Through municipal grants and public fundraising, this association bought and equipped Canada's first "rest home" for returning soldiers unable to adapt to civilian life immediately. Located at 113 David Street overlooking Victoria Park, the home provided both rest and recuperation. Raising the flag on opening day, May 9, 1917, is Col. L.W. Shannon from Military District No. 1 in London. (Courtesy WHS.)

During the slow but steady approach to war in the late 1930s, little evidence of the tension and mistrust of 1915–1917 surfaced. By 1940, it seemed everyone wanted to "take a shot at Hitler," almost everyone, that is. James White, who operated this bow-and-arrow money-raising scheme, found an anonymous note on June 10 telling him to stop or "Mr. Hitler [will] fix you when he come to Canada." It was a weak echo of the hatred of 25 years earlier. John English and Ken McLaughlin compare the two eras in their book *Kitchener: An Illustrated History*, writing, "The First World War divided Berlin and isolated it: the Second World War renewed Kitchener and drew it closer to the national economy and national mood." (Courtesy *Record*.)

The most concrete evidence of war footing was the spring 1940 construction of a military training camp at Knollwood Park behind Sheppard Public School. No. 10 Reserve Training Centre included a large drill hall, lecture rooms, soldiers' quarters, mess halls, and parade grounds. Originally to train men, the centre was altered in October 1942, emerging as No. 3 Canadian Women's Army Corps (CWAC) Basic Training Centre. (Courtesy *Record*, UW.)

In the Canadian Women's Army Corps camp, young women from across the country underwent about five weeks of physical training, drill, first-aid, and trades courses, plus clerking classes at the collegiate institute and detailed instruction in driving and mechanics at a downtown Kitchener garage. Usually, a woman was then assigned to a military base closer to her hometown. The idea was that CWACs would release men for overseas duty. Only about 10 percent of CWACs themselves went overseas. In August 1943, the corps celebrated its second birthday with a weekend festival. After a parade, sports, and exhibitions in Victoria Park on Saturday, religious services, drills, and inspections were held Sunday at Knollwood. No. 3 Canadian Women's Army Corps Training Centre closed in fall 1946. The barracks buildings were used as post-war housing for a few years, then for militia training, and were gradually pulled down over the years. (Courtesy WHS, Farrow.)

During the war, military convoys rumbled through the city, moving troops from camp to camp in southern Ontario, taking them on training exercises, or even attempting to serve as morale-boosters. This early-1940s Royal Canadian Army Service Corps truckload of troops leads a variety of military vehicles past the Red Indian service station at King East and Grove (later Kent). (Courtesy KPL.)

Once again, Kitchener's young men and women were overseas. In the midst of war, surprise meetings and reunions often occurred. In Foggia, Italy, 614 Squadron's Robert Mills (right) encountered one of those wartime coincidences when another Kitchener boy, Bruce Prange (kneeling), was assigned to 614 in the summer of 1944. The pair finished its Pathfinder squadron missions and remained friends back home for many years. Below, YMCA Supervisor Don McLaren gathered Kitchener-Waterloo men of Canadian 6 Bombing Group at Harrogate, Yorkshire. From left to right are the following: (front row) Carl Wilhelm, Irv Wismer, Bobby Bauer, Woody Dumart, Jim Craven, Willard Hallman, Bill Weicker, and Hosty Hostetler; (middle row) Ray Dedels, Bill Washburn, Don Weigand, Bill Hainsworth, Bud Copperson, Joe Cressman, Ross Huber, and Jack Yanke; (back row) Gord Thompson, Wray Easson, Len Pinke, Mack Zimmer, Milt Schmidt, Charles Arsted, Bill Field, Hank Hable, Russ Hawson, and Don McLaren. (Above, courtesy Bob Mills; below, courtesy WHS.)

SCENES OF DEVASTATION AFTER RAID ON KITCHENER

The photo at left above shows how King Street in Kitchener, looking west from Queen Street, appeared shortly after dawn this morning following last night's bombing of the Twin City by a fleet of planes believed to be Japanese. Several large craters were gouged out of the street, one of which appears in the foreground above. Hardly a building escaped damage under the savage 30-minute pounding of Axis bombs. City officials estimate that many of them, probably a majority, can be repaired in from one to four months, but several are merely empty shells and will have to be torn down. Fires continued to blaze in the wreckage until noon today, when they were brought under control. Smoke can be seen in the

On the home front, several national loan campaigns and local fundraisers kept citizens reaching for their wallets. During the 1942 Third Victory Loan Drive, the *Kitchener Daily Record* startled readers with photographs of King Street after a sneak attack by Japanese planes. A detailed story lent credence until the line "Space donated by Waterloo Trust" revealed the ruse. (Author's collection, courtesy *Record*.)

When the war in Europe ended, Kitchener paid tribute on May 20, 1945, in Victoria Park. As the honour roll of 144 Kitchener dead was read, the crowd of 10,000—in fact, the whole city—was silent. Taking the salute was Victoria Cross winner Lt. Col. David Currie. Less than a year earlier at the village of St. Lambert-sur-Dives in France, his small force delayed the escape of a large German unit. The subsequent photograph of a gaunt Currie supervising the surrendering enemy is perhaps the most famous Canadian war photograph. In Victoria Park, he stands beside W.R. Bailey of the Canadian Legion. (Courtesy WHS, Moffett.)

Eleven
ANY EXCUSE FOR A PARADE

A ribbon from an 1880s emancipation carnival, commemorative envelopes from two 1890s celebrations, and a parking decal from 1954 show that throughout its history, this community liked nothing better than a good party. From the Friedensfest to the Saengerfests and Kirmes and from historical anniversaries right up to today's Multi-Cultural Festival and Oktoberfest, the community's urge to celebrate has never slackened. (Courtesy Harold Russell, ribbon; Bob Vogel, envelopes; and Dave Moore, decal.)

Berlin had partied before 1906. The 1871 Friedensfest celebrated town status along with the German victory in the Franco-Prussian war; the huge 1880s Saengerfests featured music, and the grand opening of Victoria Park in 1896 included a whole day of celebration. But the 1906 Old Boys and Girls Reunion triumphantly proclaimed 100 years of the community and its people. In 1806, Benjamin Eby had first settled on land that developed into Berlin. Sports, music, fireworks, a Made-in-Berlin exhibition, and vaudeville artists welcomed former residents from across the continent. Most arrived at the town's still-new Grand Trunk Railway station (below), where familiar faces awaited. (Above, courtesy Nancy Zurbrigg; below, author's collection.)

This 1906 view looks towards the Walper Hotel from King Street East as Hamilton's 13th Regiment Band entertains. "Willie We Have Missed You" reads the banner posted by William Lyon Mackenzie King's friends to mark his first public visit to Berlin since 1891. King was not yet a politician but had become a prominent civil servant. (Courtesy WHS, Marion Roes.)

Four years later, Berlin celebrated again, and this bicycle was part of the reason. Daniel B. Detweiler was born in 1860 in Roseville, just south of Berlin. In 1901, he joined his brother Noah's firm, Oberholtzer Shoes (see page 37). But D.B. was no businessman; he was a promoter, a dreamer, a statesman. Among his many projects, the one that stands out is his relentless promotion of a Western Ontario Power Commission distributing Niagara Falls hydroelectric power as cheaply as possible. Opponents jeered and ridiculed; Daniel peddled and pedalled. He took his ideas from Brantford and Paris to Guelph and Elmira and to Listowel and Stratford. Detweiler's bicycle leaned against many a farmer's fence as he explained and urged the scheme. Detweiler's "Committee-of-One" gathered ideas, costs, and information throughout 1902. With E.W.B. Snider of St. Jacobs, he prepared the report from which flowed Ontario Hydro. He gave power to the people! The famous bicycle is now part of the Doon Heritage Crossroads collection. (Courtesy WHS.)

Eight years of political difficulties lay ahead before Niagara Falls hydropower lit up Ontario. The government of Sir James Whitney declared that Berlin would be the first to officially receive hydroelectricity because of its role in promoting the concept of municipalities acting co-operatively. First, an infrastructure had to be built; hundreds of kilometres of transmission lines and scores of transformer stations went up. More than 200 newspapers sent reporters to the party on October 11, 1910. Berlin was decorated with 25,000 lights, and this archway in front of the town hall (above) said "For the People" on the other side. New electric street lamps were erected along major streets, and displays of electrical appliances were set up. In the afternoon, the crowd welcomed Sir James Whitney, Sir Adam Beck, Snider, Detweiler, Mayor Charles Hahn, and other dignitaries. In the auditorium, when Beck and Whitney pressed the button at 3:30, nothing happened for a split second until manager Charles Sheppard (left) threw the main switch at the Factory Road (West Avenue) transformer station. Berlin lit up, and everyone celebrated. (Courtesy KPL.)

Two years after the hydropower celebration, Berlin threw an even larger party. The town officially became a city on June 10, 1912, and the celebrations took up a whole week in July. Parades, music, sports, a midway, speeches, and fireworks were scheduled, but what really grabbed the city's attention was the first local appearance of an airplane and aviator. Capt. Thomas Baldwin of New York, his dashing 19-year-old pilot Cecil Peoli, and the 60-horsepower Baldwin biplane were hired by the cityhood committee. Thousands crowded Brubacher's farm in the Knollwood Park area to watch the daring young man take his $5,000 machine as high as 1,000 metres into what he called the worst winds in which he had ever flown. (Author's collection, courtesy Margaret Farrow.)

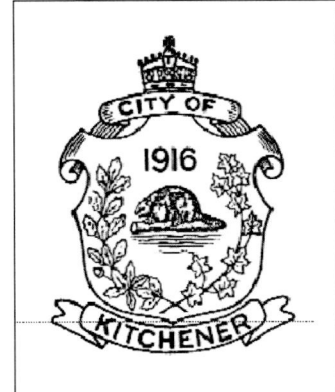

The last mayor of the town was also the first mayor of the city: W.H. Schmalz (see page 16). Schmalz was also a talented artist, calligrapher, and designer. Until 1912, the village and town had used a square seal with a crest, the date of 1854, and four symbols: a beaver, a train, a crown, and an anvil. Schmalz's cityhood celebration logo gives much information in a simple design, a design very similar to his city of Berlin crest. He kept the beaver, so symbolic of the Busy Berlin spirit, put the crown prominently at the top, and included the name and date of cityhood. Four years later, the crest had to be changed to Kitchener. Curiously, the date was also altered, and the beaver was made a little less ratlike. (Author's collection, courtesy Margaret Farrow and Bob Vogel.)

Parades were popular again in 1925 when Kitchener held its first Old Boys and Girls Reunion. This time, however, there was no special anniversary. The event was held to simply show off the city and its rapid growth and to spotlight its new city hall (to the left). Former residents from all over North America returned home between August 1 and 8 to renew old friendships. The most famous former resident was now prime minister, and William Lyon Mackenzie King did not disappoint (see page 25). He shook hands, attended banquets, made speeches, met old pals, visited his Benton Street birthplace, unveiled a portrait of himself at city hall, and made most Kitchener citizens feel proud. Businesses from the Twin Cities sponsored floats; Dominion Life's featured an armoured knight and palm trees. Below, George Ziegler leads Kitchener Musical Society musicians down King Street in their Scots Fusiliers uniforms. The Walper at the left groans under the weight of all the bunting, flags, and decorations. (Both above, courtesy WHS; below, author's collection, courtesy John Ziegler.)

On occasion, parades were not all glitz and good feelings. Through the late 1930s and early 1940s, Kitchener was beset by labour troubles as manufacturers resisted demands to bargain with employees. One thousand three-hundred rubber workers were out on February 18, 1939 when this parade of strikers wound its way past the corner of King and Queen Streets to a mass meeting at the Capitol Theatre. Edgar Dubrick, one of the striking workers, is shown in the white hat and scarf directly in front of the policeman. Within months, when war orders began pouring in and labour shortages loomed, the two sides managed to cooperate. (Courtesy KPL, *Record*.)

A decade earlier, as the Great Depression hit even prosperous and diversified cities such as Kitchener, people were often in the streets for reasons much deeper than celebrating. A group of Kitchener's unemployed workers joined the June 1936 Hunger March on Toronto and are seen parading through Hamilton on their way to Queen's Park. (Courtesy WHS, NAC.)

Although the name is unknown, sometime in 1853, Berlin's 1,000th inhabitant was born or moved here. That qualified the settlement to apply for a village charter. The first council was elected and sat in January 1854 with Dr. John Scott as reeve. One hundred years later, with villagehood and townhood long behind, the city of Kitchener put on another party: a 100th birthday party. Once again, businesses, churches, unions, service clubs, and schools put their creative touches to work on parade floats. Kitchener Packers (see page 47) used an old-world theme reflecting the owner's Polish roots. Shops and businesses along King Street were decorated, and flags waved from every pole. (Photograph by Albert Schmid; courtesy KPL.)

Mayor Donald Weber prepares to cut the cake and eat it too. Girl Scouts distributed pieces to guests attending the centennial's official opening on June 28, 1954, at city hall. Only later was it revealed to be a show cake. Another, identical in size and shape, was the real cake served to the crowd. This one was used throughout the centennial as a showpiece. Ontario Lt.-Gov. Louis O. Breithaupt, a former mayor and former MP (see page 61), returned to officially open the festivities. (Courtesy WHS, *Record*.)

In this May 1960 photograph, city hall is just out of frame to the lower right. Across King and up half a block is a scar: the cleared location of the $1.5 million fire in December 1959 (see page 68). The site of William Lyon Mackenzie King's 1874 birth is at the bottom left where the rectangular, dark building squats. Victoria Park and Victoria Public School's decorative tower are at the top left edge. In the left background is the Dominion Rubber plant on Strange Street (see page 43). (Courtesy WHS, Hunting Survey Company of Toronto.)

* * *

The journey: 1880–1960. In 1960, the downtown still holds sway over the community's commercial life but is on the verge of losing that dominance. Suburbs spread to the horizon, the new shopping malls and industrial zones spring up on the outskirts; roads are designed to move people past the downtown, and people are now willing to drive to other shopping areas, even other communities. Just over a dozen years from 1960, the focus of downtown will be lost when city hall is demolished. The year 1960 is a good time to end this "snapshot in pictures" of Berlin-Kitchener, Ontario.

Acknowledgments

Captions feature the name of the lender or a short form credit for the archival source.

WHS: Waterloo Historical Society. Formed in 1912, the society documents and archives material of old Waterloo County and current Waterloo Region. Its collection is located at the Grace Schmidt Room, Kitchener Public Library, 85 Queen Street North, Kitchener, N2H 2H1.

KPL: Kitchener Public Library. The library contains the Grace Schmidt Room of local history, where its large photograph collection of Kitchener-area photographs is kept. WHS and KPL collections are under the supervision of archivist Susan Hoffman, whose support, encouragement, and assistance to the author are beyond repayment.

BHC, UW: The University of Waterloo Library's archive of local history maintains several large collections at the Doris Lewis Rare Book Room. The Breithaupt Hewetson Clark Collection contains, in part, photographs from one of Kitchener's most prominent families, the Breithaupts.

Record, UW: The massive collection of negatives taken by the Record staff (previously the Kitchener Daily Record and the Kitchener-Waterloo Record) from the 1930s to 1997 is maintained at the Doris Lewis Rare Book Room. There are also many historical photographs accumulated by the Record kept at the University of Waterloo. For access to, information about, and unfailing assistance with the various University of Waterloo collections, I am grateful to Susan Saunders Bellingham and the staff.

Kaufman Collection, UW: After Kaufman Footwear closed in 2000, the Kitchener Industrial Artifacts Project arranged to donate Kaufman documents and photographs to the University of Waterloo. Through the kindness of the Doris Lewis Rare Book Room staff, I was able to use three images from that new collection.

Record: The Record has a collection of historical photographs in its reference library—some not in the University of Waterloo holdings. Many photographs in other archives and in private hands originated at the Record. Where obvious, I credited the Record after the lending source.

NAC: The National Archives of Canada include a huge collection of photographs, a few of which I have used where noted to provide views not available locally.

VPHC: The Victoria Park Historical Committee is a group of volunteers, including the author, who share an interest in Victoria Park and the downtown. In co-operation with the city of Kitchener, it operates a museum in the park and maintains a Victoria Park archive.

Sokvitne, Moffett, Farrow: In recent months, three women have donated remarkable family photographs and documents to the Waterloo Historical Society. Miriam Snyder Sokvitne is a direct descendant of pioneer Joseph Schneider. Photographs used here are from 1905 to 1920 albums compiled by her father, Joseph M., her uncle Albert, and her cousin Viola Snyder. Corinne Bailey Moffett is the daughter of Wilbert "Bill" Bailey, who appears several times in this book. Margaret Farrow is the granddaughter of W.G. Cleghorn, the prominent Berlin businessman, sportsman, and politician. From her father, Albert Fuller, and her grandfather, Margaret inherited two generations' worth of photographs and documents. She has now added to the gift of a third generation.

KIAP: The Kitchener Industrial Artifacts Project, under director Nicholas Rees, rescues documents, photographs, accounts, and artifacts from local businesses that close. Among KIAP successes is the donation of W.G. & R. and Arrow Shirt items to the Kitchener Public Library.

The author thanks all who loaned photographs and provided information. They are noted in the captions. A special debt is owed to friends Dave and Sandy Moore, Bob Vogel, Rob Glover, Betty and Herb Schneider, Rod Hay, Harold Russell, Laverne Hett, and Geoff Hayes. Thanks go to my dad for his patient explanations, to my co-workers, and to my employer KOOL FM and Oldies 1090.

Further thanks go to Brian Clark and the Record for permission to use the newspaper's photographs. Many of those included here were taken by the paper's first and, for many years, only staff photographer, Harry Huehnergard. He began in 1939 and set up the Record's first darkroom seven years later. In the 1950s, other photographers began working at the Record, including Mel Riepert, Al Butler, Doug Stuebing, and Joe Fehrenbach.